GLOBALVIEWPOINTS

Child Soldiers

Other Books of Related Interest:

At Issue Series

Slavery Today

Current Controversies Series

Aid to Africa

The Arms Trade

Human Trafficking

Issues in Adoption

Global Viewpoints Series

Child Labor

Slavery

Opposing Viewpoints Series

Refugees

GLOBALVIEWPOINTS

Child Soldiers

Candice Mancini, Book Editor

GREENHAVEN PRESS
A part of Gale, Cengage Learning

GALE
CENGAGE Learning™

Detroit • New York • San Francisco • New Haven, Conn • Waterville, Maine • London

Christine Nasso, *Publisher*
Elizabeth Des Chenes, *Managing Editor*

© 2010 Greenhaven Press, a part of Gale, Cengage Learning

For more information, contact:
Greenhaven Press
27500 Drake Rd.
Farmington Hills, MI 48331-3535
Or you can visit our Internet site at gale.cengage.com

For product information and technology assistance, contact us at

Gale Customer Support, 1-800-877-4253
For permission to use material from this text or product, submit all requests online at www.cengage.com/permissions

Further permissions questions can be emailed to permissionrequest@cengage.com

Articles in Greenhaven Press anthologies are often edited for length to meet page requirements. In addition, original titles of these works are changed to clearly present the main thesis and to explicitly indicate the author's opinion. Every effort is made to ensure that Greenhaven Press accurately reflects the original intent of the authors. Every effort has been made to trace the owners of copyrighted material.

LIBRARY OF CONGRESS CATALOGING-IN-PUBLICATION DATA

Child soldiers / Candice Mancini, book editor.
    p. cm. -- (Global viewpoints)
  Includes bibliographical references and index.
  ISBN 978-0-7377-4839-0 (hardcover) -- ISBN 978-0-7377-4840-6 (pbk.)
  1. Child soldiers--Juvenile literature. I. Mancini, Candice.
  UB416.C478 2010
  355.3083--dc22
                                                          2009045724

Printed in the United States of America
1 2 3 4 5 6 7 14 13 12 11 10

Contents

Foreword   **11**

Introduction   **14**

Chapter 1: The Global Problem of Child Soldiers

1. Child Soldiers Are Found Throughout   **19**
the World

Mirjana Rakela

Around the world child soldiers are manipulated by
armed groups. It is estimated that there are three hundred thousand child soldiers; most are between the ages
of fourteen and eighteen, although many are as young as
nine.

2. In **Uganda**, the Child Soldier Situation   **27**
Has Reached Crisis Status

Namrita Talwar

Approximately thirty thousand children have been abducted by the Lord's Resistance Army (LRA) in Uganda
to aid in the eighteen-year-old rebellion against the government. Discontinuing the horrible practice is a considerable challenge.

3. In **Mozambique**, Children Are Exploited   **33**
as the Perfect Weapon

Jeffrey Gettleman

Although child soldiers are not unique to Africa, Africa's
child soldiers face an unprecedented number of movements that exploit them for their innocence.

4. **Colombian** Peace Is Challenged by   **39**
an Abundance of Child Soldiers

Charles Geisler and Niousha Roshani

In Colombia the growing number of internally displaced
persons (IDPs) contributes to the growing number of
child soldiers.

5. The **United States** Treats Captured Child   48
Soldiers as if They Are Criminals
Vincent J. Curtis

According to the United Nations, the United States must
treat child soldiers as if they are victims, not criminals.
The United States holds a child soldier captured in Afghanistan at Guantánamo Bay.

6. Young Girls Are Soldiers, Too   54
Susan McKay

Although their experiences may be similar, girl soldiers
suffer differently than boy soldiers. Unlike boys, girls are
regularly sexually exploited.

Periodical Bibliography   61

Chapter 2: The Causes and Effects of Children in Combat

1. Threats and Promises Entice Children to War   63
P.W. Singer

Children living in war zones are enticed into war by
threats and promises of food, shelter, and group accep-
tance. Even those who "volunteer" are coerced to join by
their desperate needs.

2. **Democratic Republic of the Congo**'s   74
Forgotten Children of Conflict
Anushka Asthana

Two years after fighting for a rebel army group in the
Democratic Republic of the Congo, former child soldiers
want to return home. But their families and communities say they do not want them back.

3. Modern Child Soldiers Have Unique   83
Health Concerns
J. Pearn

Child soldiers suffer from unique health hazards. These
include death, violence-related injuries, and serious mental health illnesses.

4. Former Child Soldiers Benefit from Indigenous   **96**
   Cultural Practices of Healing
   Zulfiya Tursunova

   In war-ravaged countries that use child soldiers, Western
   approaches to reintegration dominate. But indigenous
   healing rituals must be recognized as valid as well.

5. **Colombia**'s Child Soldiers Join Rebels   **106**
   to Escape Poverty
   Helen Murphy

   In Colombia poverty drives countless children to join the
   Revolutionary Armed Forces of Colombia (FARC), even
   though the only escape is through death.

6. In **Iraq**, Child Soldiers Want to Be Martyrs   **113**
   Toby Harnden

   In Iraq children who fight think American soldiers are
   weak and lacking in faith. These children want to live
   victoriously or meet a glorious death.

Periodical Bibliography   **118**

Chapter 3: Efforts to End the Use of Children as Soldiers

1. International Efforts to Combat Child Soldiers   **120**
   Are Not Enough
   UN General Assembly, Social, Humanitarian,
   and Cultural Affairs Committee

   Despite international efforts to eliminate the use of children as soldiers, children continue to be victimized by
   conflict. This contributes to the overall state of violence
   and poverty these children endure.

2. **Africa** Must Stop Recruiting Children to War   **131**
   Ernest Harsch

   At the Free Children from War conference in Paris,
   French Foreign Minister Philippe Douste-Blazy warned
   that the use of child soldiers is a threat to Africa and to
   the international community. Former child soldier Ishmael Beah, speaking at the conference, affirmed.

3. **British** Relief Organization Offers Aid to   **136**
   Children Affected by War in **Sierra Leone**
   Lindsay Clydesdale

   In Sierra Leone an eleven-year war left fifty thousand
   dead, one hundred thousand mutilated, and countless
   child soldiers psychologically damaged. A British charity
   organization, Comic Relief, offers help.

4. In **Mozambique**, Save the Children Helps   **142**
   Child Soldiers Heal
   Wray Herbert

   The international aid organization Save the Children
   helped former child soldiers in a Mozambique orphanage. Other local factors contributed to their well-being,
   also.

5. Despite International Efforts, Child Soldiers   **155**
   Continue to Be Used in Battle
   Coalition to Stop the Use of Child Soldiers

   International efforts to end the use of child soldiers have
   made some progress, but have not done nearly enough.
   And even in the United Kingdom and the United States,
   peacetime armies recruit children under the age of eighteen.

Periodical Bibliography   **162**

Chapter 4: Life After Combat

1. Former **Cambodian** Child Soldier Finds   **164**
   Solace in Writing
   Susan Mansfield

   Loung Ung's recovery from the horrors of being a child
   soldier did not begin once she moved to America; recovery began once she started to write.

2. Former **Ugandan** Child Soldier Helps   **171**
   Others Experience Childhood
   Edd McCracken

   China Keitetsi's lost childhood and life with a gun made
   her a fighter. Having escaped Uganda and the National
   Resistance Army, she now fights to save other child soldiers.

3. Former Child Soldier from **Democratic Republic of the Congo** Now Works as a Carpenter   177

Bent Jorgen Perlmutt

After serving as a spy for a year and seeing atrocities done to his friends and village, Maisha escaped from the Mayi-Mayi militia that he had joined at age fifteen. He went through a UNICEF reintegration program and eventually learned the carpentry trade.

4. Former Child Soldier from **Sierra Leone** Is Now Author and Child Rights Advocate   181

Naveed Malik, interviewing Ishmael Beah

Ishmael Beah's experience as a child soldier is well-known from his memoir *A Long Way Gone: Memoirs of a Boy Soldier*. Now living in New York, Beah works for Human Rights Watch.

Periodical Bibliography   189

For Further Discussion   190

Organizations to Contact   192

Bibliography of Books   197

Index   200

Foreword

"The problems of all of humanity can only be solved by all of humanity."
—Swiss author Friedrich Dürrenmatt

Global interdependence has become an undeniable reality. Mass media and technology have increased worldwide access to information and created a society of global citizens. Understanding and navigating this global community is a challenge, requiring a high degree of information literacy and a new level of learning sophistication.

Building on the success of its flagship series, *Opposing Viewpoints*, Greenhaven Press has created the *Global Viewpoints* series to examine a broad range of current, often controversial topics of worldwide importance from a variety of international perspectives. Providing students and other readers with the information they need to explore global connections and think critically about worldwide implications, each *Global Viewpoints* volume offers a panoramic view of a topic of widespread significance.

Drugs, famine, immigration—a broad, international treatment is essential to do justice to social, environmental, health, and political issues such as these. Junior high, high school, and early college students, as well as general readers, can all use *Global Viewpoints* anthologies to discern the complexities relating to each issue. Readers will be able to examine unique national perspectives while, at the same time, appreciating the interconnectedness that global priorities bring to all nations and cultures.

Material in each volume is selected from a diverse range of sources, including journals, magazines, newspapers, nonfiction books, speeches, government documents, pamphlets, organization newsletters, and position papers. *Global Viewpoints* is truly global, with material drawn primarily from international sources available in English and secondarily from U.S. sources with extensive international coverage.

Features of each volume in the *Global Viewpoints* series include:

- An **annotated table of contents** that provides a brief summary of each essay in the volume, including the name of the country or area covered in the essay.

- An **introduction** specific to the volume topic.

- A **world map** to help readers locate the countries or areas covered in the essays.

- For each viewpoint, an **introduction** that contains notes about the author and source of the viewpoint explains why material from the specific country is being presented, summarizes the main points of the viewpoint, and offers three **guided reading questions** to aid in understanding and comprehension.

- **For further discussion** questions that promote critical thinking by asking the reader to compare and contrast aspects of the viewpoints or draw conclusions about perspectives and arguments.

- A worldwide list of **organizations to contact** for readers seeking additional information.

- A **periodical bibliography** for each chapter and a **bibliography of books** on the volume topic to aid in further research.

- A comprehensive **subject index** to offer access to people, places, events, and subjects cited in the text, with the countries covered in the viewpoints highlighted.

Global Viewpoints is designed for a broad spectrum of readers who want to learn more about current events, history, political science, government, international relations, economics, environmental science, world cultures, and sociology—students doing research for class assignments or debates, teachers and faculty seeking to supplement course materials, and others wanting to understand current issues better. By presenting how people in various countries perceive the root causes, current consequences, and proposed solutions to worldwide challenges, *Global Viewpoints* volumes offer readers opportunities to enhance their global awareness and their knowledge of cultures worldwide.

Introduction

The United Nations Convention on the Rights of the Child defines a child as "a person below the age of eighteen, unless the laws of a particular country set the legal age for adulthood younger." Such ambiguity reflects the complexity of the situation, and brings to mind some vital questions. Does a true definition of "child," spanning each and every society, exist? Does culture influence how "adult" and "child" are differentiated? Has the perception of "childhood" changed throughout history?

It is likely that the increase in life expectancy in many nations has changed perceptions of childhood. In the United States, life expectancy increased from forty-nine in 1900 to seventy-eight in 2007. Using the under-eighteen definition of childhood, this reflects an increase in adulthood by twenty-nine years. Given this definition, in 1900 the average person lived eighteen years as a child and thirty-one years as an adult; in 2007 this equaled eighteen years as a child and sixty years as an adult. It seems logical that as adult years were extended, there would be a desire to extend childhood years. In contrast, when adult years have been relatively short, an extended childhood might have seemed an unaffordable luxury, especially in situations where food and other life necessities have been in short supply.

In 1900 large numbers of children from the United States and other industrialized nations worked throughout the laboring industry in mines, factories, and canneries. In the United States, these child laborers were the children of men who as boys may have participated in the Civil War. Boys under the age of eighteen were common in the Union and Confederate ranks, especially among drum and bugle corps. Earlier, children participated in the Napoleonic Wars (1803–1815), the American Revolutionary War (1775–1783), and France's Hundred Years' War (1337–1453).

Historically, male youth were expected to be brave, strong, and skilled warriors. The great warrior of the Trojan War, Achilles, among the greatest of Greek heroes, was thought to have been fifteen when he sailed off to Troy. To the ancient Greeks, and later the Romans, for a male to die without honor was disastrous and to die with glory was ideal. Because of the dominant hero culture that existed—perpetuated by epic tales such as *The Iliad*—and likely because the average life expectancy of ancient Greeks was around thirty years old, fears of dying young were less pressing than fears of dying unremembered. The great Greek hero Theseus embodied this belief. Theseus's father, King Aegeus, left him when he was in his mother's womb, leaving a sword and sandals under a very heavy stone. The king advised Theseus's mother to send the boy to him once he was strong enough to lift the stone to gather the gifts. As a youth, Theseus lifted the rock, and thus established his hero reputation when he set out with his sword on a long and dangerous land voyage (refusing to take the easier path on boat), where he battled many monsters and won. According to legend, Theseus's role model, Hercules, killed two deadly snakes with his bare hands as an infant. As a teenager, Hercules single-handedly slayed a fierce lion, and continued on this superhuman path of might into adulthood.

Of the ancient Greek city-states, Sparta best embodied the military culture, and was least likely to mourn over a sense of lost childhood. At the age of seven, male Spartan children were taken from their mothers and handed over to the state. The state trained the boys to be soldiers: Training involved intense exercise, and they were forced to endure cold, hunger, thirst, lack of sleep, pain, and hardship—many of the practices that are now identified as torture for adults and unimaginable cruelty for a child.

As people have grown to expect to live longer, the ideal of childhood has become more respected and protected. In a time and place of sixty adult years to live, eighteen childhood years might seem fair and appropriate. This conviction has begun to spread throughout the world, as evidenced by the United Nations Convention on the Rights of the Child. Through such organizations as UNICEF (United Nations International Children's Emergency Fund), Amnesty International, and Invisible Children Inc., the belief that the world needs to transition its youth from guns to education has been shifting the historical and worldwide sense of childhood. Even the great ancient Greek philosopher Plato, who expressed admiration for Sparta's discipline but distaste for its singular focus on military, believed that "no man should bring children into the world who is unwilling to persevere to the end in their nature and education."

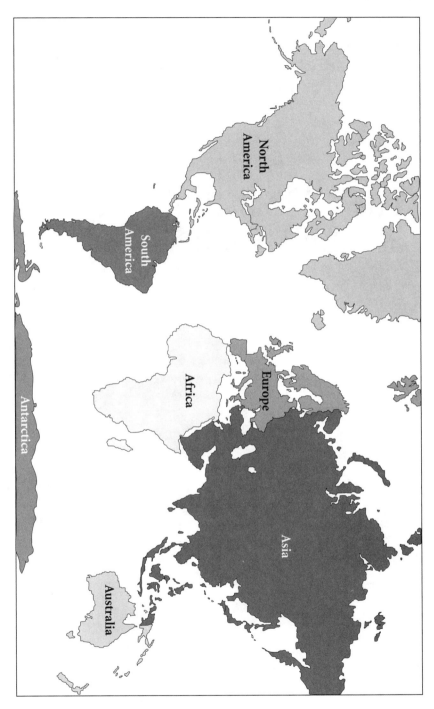

GLOBAL VIEWPOINTS

CHAPTER 1

The Global Problem of Child Soldiers

Child Soldiers Are Found Throughout the World

Mirjana Rakela

Throughout the world, child soldiers are being manipulated into joining armed forces. While a definite number cannot be determined, it is estimated that three hundred thousand children act as soldiers around the world, not only in Africa, but also in Asia, the Middle East, South America, and Europe. In the following viewpoint, Mirjana Rakela asserts that poverty is a key factor leading children to become soldiers. She explains that these children, who are often surrounded by violence, are easily manipulated and brainwashed. She calls on Western nations to take up their cause. Mirjana Rakela, a Radio Free Europe/Radio Liberty *correspondent for South Slavic and Albanian Languages Service, was the recipient of the 2008 Lorenzo Natali Journalism Prize for her reports on child soldiers, first broadcast in November 2007.*

As you read, consider the following questions:

1. According to Mirjana Rakela, what makes children more easily manipulated than adults?
2. How does poverty aid in the recruitment of child soldiers?
3. How does the Taliban convince child soldiers to carry out suicide missions?

An estimated 300,000 children are currently involved in 33 armed conflicts around the world. Nongovernmental organizations [NGOs] say about 100,000 of them live in Africa. They are usually between 14 and 18 years of age, although child soldiers as young as nine are not rare. Some are volunteers, but the vast majority of them were forcefully recruited into paramilitary and military units. They took up arms in order to survive after family, social, and economic breakdowns, often after seeing their families tortured or killed by the regime's soldiers or armed groups. Girls are not spared either. In El Salvador, Ethiopia, and Uganda, almost a third of little soldiers are girls. Increasingly modern, user-friendly military technology and weapons have made it easier for armed groups to misuse children and turn them into warriors. Once recruited, children can be used as cooks, suppliers, or guards. But more often than not, they are sent to the front line of combat, to patrol minefields, and even on suicide missions in Afghanistan, Iraq, and elsewhere.

Enrique Restoy, of the Coalition to Stop the Use of Child Soldiers, says children have fought in all known conflicts in the Middle East. He has personally met many child soldiers from regions such as the Palestinian territories, Lebanon, or Sudan. Children, he says, suffer the after-effects of war, even when they try to hide them—war memories don't fade overnight, especially if these children have committed crimes. Support programs for these children, however, are generally quick and rarely focus on long-term education and social reinsertion.

Easily Manipulated

Restoy says some children are actually proud to have served in armed groups that combated forces occupying their country. "Children in Iraq and the Palestinian territories live surrounded by violence—on one side there are armed groups, on the other the occupying army," Restoy said. "They face violence almost daily and unfortunately they have access to weapons. It's true that in some countries, like Yemen, weapons are part of the culture and very young children carry weapons as a symbol of their family's importance and prestige.

"But children are easily manipulated, and this is why we want to prohibit any kind of involvement of children in armed conflicts. They are not mature enough to decide whether or not they want, and should, belong to an armed group. Armed groups or the army recruiting them manipulate them without difficulty. And regardless of whether the children voluntarily join these groups or live in a region under occupation, there's always a crime committed by their recruiters and a manipulation committed by their recruiters."

"'A child can go anywhere without being stopped by soldiers and policemen, so unfortunately they can carry out any kind of attack.'"

Diar Bamri, a correspondent for *RFE/RL*'s [*Radio Free Europe/Radio Liberty*'s] Iraqi Service, says media reports and international organizations confirm that terrorist groups in Iraq use children as militants. The *Los Angeles Times* for instance, citing U.S. sources, reported in 2007 that some 800 children suspected of carrying out terrorist attacks were jailed in U.S. prisons in Iraq, some as young as 11 years old.

Poverty Creates Child Soldiers

Poverty is a key factor pushing children to enroll as fighters. "I think one of the reasons is money. Many come from very poor families, they have lost their fathers and brothers. These families need money because they don't have any regular income. They ask children to go out on the streets and bring money home, they don't ask where this money comes from," Bamri says. "They tell them to drop out of school because the time is for survival, not education. On the streets, children become easy prey for terrorists and organized groups that re-cruit them. A child can go anywhere without being stopped by soldiers and policemen, so unfortunately they can carry out any kind of attack.

"Such children do not differ from other children on the street, and there are many thousands of them wandering around Iraqi cities. Who can determine whether a child is good or bad, whether or not he is a terrorist? When you speak to these boys, they tell you: 'I was manipulated, used, forced because our family is very poor.' Terrorist groups like al Qaeda pay these children up to $300 a month. By comparison, an av-erage Iraqi family today survives on $100 to $150 a month. That's why these children are ready to do anything for money."

State of Fear

The testimonials published by Human Rights Watch are shock-ing. Emilio, recruited into the Guatemalan army when he was 14 years old, recalls how child soldiers were constantly beaten up into a state of permanent fear. They were more often hun-gry than sated [full], they had to carry heavy armament. They were taught to fight against enemies in a war they didn't un-derstand.

Susan, a 16-year-old from Uganda, tells the story of a boy from her village who tried to escape after being abducted and recruited into the Lord's Resistance Army. He was captured, and the other children were forced to beat him to death with hoes. After they had killed him, they were ordered to smear their own hands with his blood, to overcome their fear of death and dissuade them from escaping.

Following the latest wave of violence in Burma, Human Rights Watch published a report detailing how the military re-gime in this Asian country recruits children into their armed forces. Jo Becker, who works at Human Rights Watch's New York headquarters, says the Burmese army is recruiting thou-sands of children into its forces. "The army is constantly increasing its number of battalions, but at the same time there are more and more deserters. The armed forces have trouble meeting recruitment quotas, so they realized that children make an easy target. They approach them on the street, in public places, and force them to join the army," Becker says. "Children have told us that they are beaten when they are not able to endure military drills. They frequently try to escape, but when they are captured and taken back to the recruitment center, they are beaten by their colleagues. In some cases they are severely injured, some even die. We spoke to about 20 former soldiers. The majority of them were recruited when they were 10 years old.

"Three of the former soldiers we spoke to were recruited twice. One of them was first recruited when he was 14 years old. He managed to escape the following year, but he was captured. When his grandmother and aunt realized that he was back in the army, they traveled to his unit and asked the commander to release him. The man said: 'I will let him go, but only if you bring me five other recruits in exchange.' When the boy found this out, he told his aunt: 'Don't do that, don't bring five other people. Life here is terrible and I have to face it myself.' Afterwards, he started voluntarily signing up for the most dangerous assignments. What he said to us was: 'In the army, my life was worthless.'"

Unknown Numbers of Child Soldiers

The director of *RFE/RL*'s North Caucasus Service, Aslan Doukaev, says there is no precise figure for the number of child fighters in the region. But rights groups say a great number of minors are definitely involved in fighting in the North Caucasus. "I saw with my own eyes how a boy who was 13 or 14 at most grabbed a gun from a Russian paramilitary soldier in the center of Grozny, on a marketplace, and killed him. Children try to get hold of weapons in order to join military groups," Doukaev says.

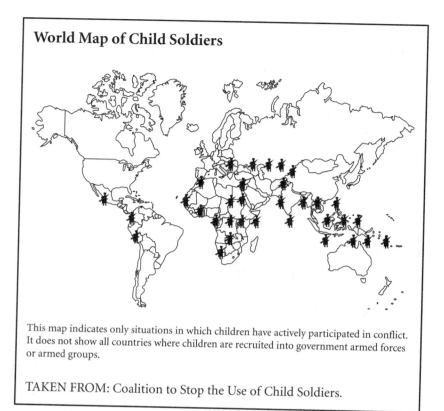

World Map of Child Soldiers

This map indicates only situations in which children have actively participated in conflict. It does not show all countries where children are recruited into government armed forces or armed groups.

TAKEN FROM: Coalition to Stop the Use of Child Soldiers.

"I also know that some of them are real experts in planting mines and traps. But there is no organized campaign to recruit children. This often happens spontaneously. Some children don't have parents, others come from poor or destroyed families, and joining militant fighters makes them feel important and significant. Schools are either closed or function poorly, kids have nowhere to go. They have a choice between staying at home and risking being arrested, exposed to violence and drugs; or join one of the military groups. Very often, they choose the second option."

The number of children fighting in Afghanistan is not known either; international organizations say the Taliban and al Qaeda have thousands of boys in their ranks. Their number has been declining in recent years. But Mohammad Amin

Mudaqiq, the director of *RFE/RL*'s Kabul bureau, says the insurgents are still recruiting children.

"The Talibans usually enroll teenagers, children aged 13 to 14. Some are even younger, but they prepare all of them equally for suicide missions. Al Qaeda and the Talibans take advantage of the fact that high-ranking state officials are usually happy to meet children. Children are easily brainwashed and led to believe that after the suicide attack, they will go to heaven," Mudaqiq says.

"We know of a boy who was recruited as a suicide bomber but then changed his mind and decided to surrender to authorities. He called his father from Pakistan to ask him for forgiveness, and the father forgave him publicly. A child was used as a human shield in a recent suicide attack in Baghlan that killed around 80 people. The bomber walked behind the child, who approached a member of parliament with a bunch of flowers. Security forces let the child and the older person through, and when they were close to the deputy the suicide bomber detonated the explosive. Insurgents recently also used students from the madrasah [Muslim school] in order to approach NATO [North Atlantic Treaty Organization] soldiers in Kabul and attack them. NATO soldiers fired in retaliation, and 12 children died."

"'Children are easily brainwashed and led to believe that after the suicide attack, they will go to heaven.'"

European Problem

In Europe, too, children have been drawn into armed conflicts—the 1990s Balkan wars are the most recent example. The UN [United Nations] Declaration of the Rights of the Child [created in 1959] was largely ignored during the war years, and scores of children died in the fighting. The war prompted the European Union in 2003 to adopt guidelines concerning children affected by armed conflicts. The European Parliament drafted a resolution aimed at curbing the recruitment and use of children in armed conflicts. Such a document would give the European Parliament more leverage on governments, but also international bodies such as the United Nations, when calling for more measures against the use of children in armed conflicts. One of the driving forces behind the resolution was Britain's Sharon Bowles, a member of the European Parliament. Using children as soldiers, she says, is a new form of slavery.

"Quite often they are given drugs and put in the front line, their childish innocence and unpredictable behavior are used as a weapon in war. We want as many people as possible to be aware of the existence of child warriors and to have as many states as possible take part in the action, in order for the Convention on the Rights of the Child to be truly respected," Bowles says.

"I would like to emphasize that the use of children as soldiers is a new form of slavery. This is a type of forced labor in horrifying conditions. This is the worst possible form of slavery. Our goal is to have countries of the West, big nations such as the United States or Russia, exert real political pressure on countries where this is taking place. This is part of today's reality, but we have to be active in preventing it as much as possible and applying diplomatic pressure."

In Uganda, the Child Soldier Situation Has Reached Crisis Status

Namrita Talwar

By 2004, the Lord's Resistance Army's (LRA's) rebellion against the government had been ongoing for eighteen years. (The rebellion continues today.) In the following viewpoint, Namrita Talwar examines the impact those eighteen years have had on Uganda and, in particular, on Uganda's child soldiers. She provides specific details about the horrors faced by these children. Talwar is a science journalist and an associate editor at the United Nations.

As you read, consider the following questions:

1. Why do Ugandan children and mothers flee their homes to stay in overcrowded camps?
2. Why did the United Nations Security Council adopt resolution 1539 on April 22, 2004?
3. According to the journal the *Lancet*, what are some of the atrocities inflicted on child soldiers in Uganda?

For the rebels in northern Uganda, children have become their killing machines. Some are as young as eight years old when the Lord's Resistance Army (LRA) abduct and intro-

Namrita Talwar, "Fostering Terror: Child Soldier Crisis in Uganda," *UN Chronicle*, vol. 41, no. 2, June–August 2004, pp. 7–8. Copyright © 2004 United Nations. Reprinted with the permission of the United Nations. The United Nations is the author of the original material.

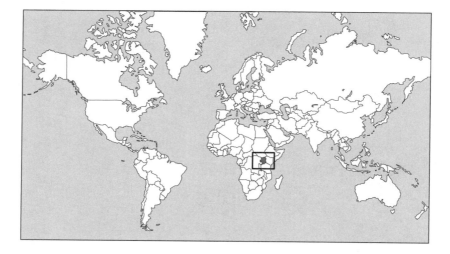

duce them to the rebellion movement. Since the 18-year-old rebellion against the government began [in 1986], some 30,000 children have been abducted to work as soldiers and porters. Young girls have been made to serve as the "wives" of rebels and bear their children. In the past 18 months [between 2003 and 2004], 10,000 children have been abducted as a result of a Ugandan military offensive against the LRA. [Editor's Note: As of 2008, it was estimated that around 3,000 abducted children remained held captive by the LRA.]

To evade the rebels and escape attacks and killings, streams of children, often with their mothers, flee their homes to squalid and overcrowded camps. Some 40,000 "night commuters" sleep under verandas, in schools, hospital courtyards and bus parking lots. The number of internally displaced persons has almost tripled since 2002. Any economic strides made by Uganda, which revitalized its gross domestic product (GDP) growth to more than 8 percent over the past three years, hangs loosely in the hands of the insurgency, threatening to undermine the country's progress. The unrest in the northern and eastern parts of Uganda has created the largest displaced populations.

Efforts to Combat the Use of Child Soldiers

In its continuing efforts to combat the growing menace of using children as soldiers, the United Nations Security Council adopted resolution 1539 (2004) on 22 April [2004], recalling States' responsibilities to "end the impunity and to prosecute those responsible for genocide, crimes against humanity, war crimes and other egregious crimes penetrated against children." The resolution also calls upon parties to "prepare within three months concrete time-bound action plans to halt recruitment and use of children in violation of the international obligations applicable to them". Under the Rome Statute of the International Criminal Court, the enlistment of children under 15 years of age or using them to participate actively in hostilities is classified as a war crime, while the Optional Protocol to the Convention on the Rights of the Child requires States parties to set a minimum age of 18 for compulsory recruitment and participation in hostilities.

Although various advances have been made for the protection of children affected by armed conflict, particularly in the areas of advocacy, the resolution notes a lack of overall "progress on the ground", where parties to the conflict continue to violate relevant provisions of the international laws aimed at protecting these children.

Despite the gravity of the situation in Uganda, less than 10 percent of the $130 million requested by the humanitarian community for 2004 has been received. In some areas, malnutrition rates as high as 30 percent have been recorded among children. Fear of rebel attacks badly hit the planting season this year, threatening to aggravate in the coming months the already severe food shortages.

Even as a peace process makes significant progress in neighbouring Sudan, the rebel faction has made peace in Uganda tenuous, representing in the minds of the world's eco-

Does "Abduction" Have a Universal Definition?

A child goes missing, abducted, in the United States. The police are notified and they issue what in America is referred to as an AMBER Alert. Radio stations begin broadcasting descriptions, while TV stations flash pictures of both the abductor and abducted across the screen. Billboards along major roads flash pertinent information regarding the abduction. The police move out in force with helicopters and planes and the Army National Guard may even be engaged. Everything is put into operation to bring a child home to its family. At the same time, they go after the abductor to put him behind bars, so she or he cannot harm any other child.

In another part of the world, on the other side of this globe, in the northern districts of Uganda, 30,000 children have been abducted in the past 20 some years. Most every family in the Acholi and now Langi area has been affected. Many families have lost a child through abduction, or their village was attacked and destroyed, families burned out and/or killed, and harvests destroyed by an army of abducted children known as the Lord's Resistance Army. The countryside is virtually empty and people have moved into safe villages that are supposed to be protected by the government, but that has often been in words but not in deed. At night the children of the north flee into towns to sleep, fearing that they might be abducted. They find safety in numbers in towns such as Gulu where even the local bishops and ministers have joined them as they seek safety from the Lord's Resistance Army.

Experience Uganda Safaris,
"Another Town in Africa—'Lira,'" July 29, 2009. http://kabiza.com.

nomic policy makers a jarring contrast with the tragedy of conflict in the north and east, which shows no signs of abating.

The Lasting Trauma of Child Soldiers

The Lord's Resistance Army, with 90 percent of its force being children, has become a classic case of the most disturbing aspect of a humanitarian crisis. Children are brutalized and forced to commit atrocities on fellow abductees and even siblings. Those who attempt to escape are killed.

A study published on 13 March 2004 by the United Kingdom–based scientific journal, the *Lancet*, reports that child soldiers who had served in the LRA rebel group and were forced to kill or watch other people being killed, may remain traumatized for years after being released. The study that surveyed some 300 former child soldiers found that over half of those abducted at an average age of twelve had been seriously beaten, 77 percent had witnessed someone being killed, 39 percent had killed another person, and 39 percent had abducted other children. Over one-third of the girls had been raped, while 18 percent had given birth while in captivity. "Since these former child soldiers are often blamed and stigmatized for the countless atrocities they committed—mostly against their own people—their psychological recovery and reintegration can be seriously complicated", according to the study.

"Children are brutalized and forced to commit atrocities on fellow abductees and even siblings. Those who attempt to escape are killed."

Of 71 children who completed a questionnaire to assess post-traumatic reactions, 69 showed clinically significant symptoms, the *Lancet* reported. Almost all of them had experienced a number of traumatic events, on average six each.

31

About 6 percent had seen their mother, father, brother or sister being killed, while 2 percent had participated in killing their father, brother or another relative, the study revealed. Over one-third of the children were found to have no mother, while two-thirds had no father.

In Mozambique, Children Are Exploited as the Perfect Weapon

Jeffrey Gettleman

In the following viewpoint, Jeffrey Gettleman argues that although Africa did not invent the modern child soldier, Africa's situation is unique. Modern leaders of armed movements in Africa are less charismatic and more brutish than in other places and times. Also, many of these leaders use talk of magic and spirits to manipulate children into doing what they want. Although the world has finally noticed the dire situation of African children in war zones, Gettleman believes much more must be done to alleviate the situation. Gettleman is the East Africa bureau chief for the New York Times.

As you read, consider the following questions:

1. How many child soldiers exist worldwide, according to human rights groups?
2. Which three countries are listed as representing Africa's longest-running conflicts?
3. Who is Ishmael Beah?

In the early 1980s, in the lowlands of Mozambique, a new technology of warfare emerged that would sweep across Africa and soon the rest of the world: the child soldier. Rebel

Jeffrey Gettleman, "Children at War, Fighting to Plunder; Greed, Not Ideology, Now Drives Conscription of African Youths," *International Herald Tribune*, April 30, 2007, p. 1. Copyright © 2007 by *International Herald Tribune*. Reprinted with permission.

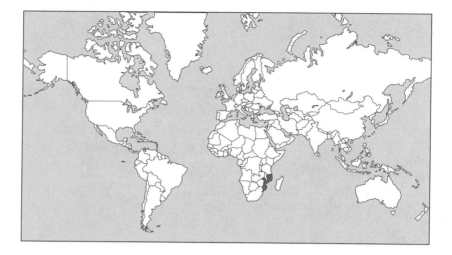

commanders had constructed a youthful killing machine that cut its way through village after village and nearly overran the government. Its trail was smoking huts and sawed-off ears. The Mozambicans learned that children were the perfect weapon: easily manipulated, intensely loyal, fearless, and most important, in endless supply.

Today [2007], human rights groups say there are 300,000 child soldiers worldwide. And experts say the problem is deepening as the nature of conflict itself changes—especially in Africa. Here, in one country after another, conflicts have morphed from idea- or cause-driven struggles to warlord-led drives whose essential goal is plunder. Because those new rebel movements are motivated and financed by crime, popular support becomes irrelevant. Those in control don't care about hearts and minds. They see the local population as prey.

Child Soldiers Found in Long-Running Conflicts

The result is that few adults want to have anything to do with them, and manipulating and abducting children becomes the best way to sustain the organized banditry. This dynamic has fueled some of the longest-running conflicts on the continent, and it could be seen this month alone in at least three countries:

In Somalia, within the last month, more than 1,000 people have been killed in Mogadishu, the capital, in a complex civil war compounded by warlords who command armies of teenagers. The war can be traced to 1991, when the central government was brought down by clans fighting over old grievances. But soon it became a contest among the warlords for control of airports, seaports and access to international aid. Sixteen years later, they are still blasting away.

In Congo, a civil war that started a decade ago to oust the Cold War–era tyrant Mobutu Sese Seko is now a multiheaded fight in which only one of the players is the government. The rest are rebel posses fighting among themselves for shares of the country's timber, copper, gold, diamonds and other resources. All sides, according to a report issued this month by Human Rights Watch, rely on child soldiers.

In Uganda, the latest in a series of peace talks—none successful so far—resumed last week in an effort to end a reign of terror in rural areas by the Lord's Resistance Army [LRA]. That group was mustered in the late 1990s in the name of the oppressed Acholi minority, but soon degenerated into a drugged-out street gang living in the jungle with military-grade weaponry and 13-year-old brides. Its ranks are filled with boys who have been brainwashed to burn down huts and pound newborn babies to death in wooden mortars, as if they were grinding grain.

The Modern Armed Movement of Africa

Africa didn't invent the modern underage soldier. The Nazis drafted adolescents when they got desperate. So did Iran, which gave boys 12 to 16 years old plastic keys to heaven to hang around their necks as they cleared minefields during the

Children Charged for Crimes They Committed Against Their Will

Children enrolled by force into armed opposition groups often have little choice but to remain and fight. In Uganda, for example, if children abducted by the LRA [Lord's Resistance Army] do manage to escape or surrender, they may face the wrath of the government. Despite claims made on Ugandan television by the armed forces that they are *"rescuing these children daily"*, and *"handing them to charity organisations for care"*, in January 1999, the Ugandan army executed, in circumstances to be clarified, five teenage boys between the ages of 14 and 17 suspected of being rebel soldiers. Moreover, in April 1998, 25 boys were charged with treason and are still awaiting trial. All these boys face the death sentence even though they were *abducted* by rebels and used as child soldiers by them. The children are charged with failing to release information about rebel soldiers or are said to have fought with the rebels. If the death penalty were carried out against these youths, this would be a manifest violation of the Geneva Conventions and their Additional Protocols and of the Convention on the Rights of the Child. These international treaties, to which Uganda is a party, clearly prohibit capital punishment for those under 18 years of age at the time of the commission of the offence.

Relief Web,
"The Use of Children as Soldiers in Africa: A Country Analysis of Child Recruitment and Participation in Armed Conflict,"
May 15, 2002. www.reliefweb.int.

Iran-Iraq War. Young teenagers have fought in religion-driven or nationalistic fights in Kosovo, the Palestinian territories and Afghanistan.

But here, in Africa, armed movements that survive on children as young as 9 have acquired a special character, nourished by breakdowns of state power or ideology. Many of these movements are about raw greed, power and brutality, with no effort to make excuses for it. "There might have been a little rhetoric at the beginning," said Ishmael Beah, a former child soldier in Sierra Leone and author of the best seller *A Long Way Gone: Memoirs of a Boy Soldier.* "But very quickly the ideology gets lost. And then it just becomes a bloodbath, a way for the commanders to plunder, a war of madness."

Neil Boothby, a Columbia University professor who has worked with child soldiers across the world, said this new crop of movements lacked the features associated with the winning insurgencies of yesteryear—a charming, intelligent leader, persuasive vocabulary, the goal of taking cities. The typical rebel leader emerging today wants most of all to run his criminal enterprise deep in the bush. "These are brutally thuggy people who don't want to rule politically and have no strategy for winning a war," Boothby said.

"Many of these movements are about raw greed, power and brutality, with no effort to make excuses for it."

This is a sharp change from the liberation movements of the 1970s and 1980s and the cause-driven conflicts that followed—for example, those in Zimbabwe or Eritrea. Even Rwanda's 1994 genocide followed some familiar patterns: It remained a contest, however gruesome, for political power between two ethnic groups. And children, by and large, were the victims of atrocities by adults, rather than the other way around.

In many armed movements, children are taught that life and death depend on spirits, which are conjured up by their commanders and distilled in oils and amulets. Magic can spur children to do unspeakable things. It also bestows otherwise lackluster leaders with a veneer of supernatural respectability. "The commanders would wear certain pearls and said that guns wouldn't hurt us," Beah recalled. "And we believed it."

Children Manipulated by "Magic"

Renamo, the South African-backed rebel army that terrorized Mozambique in the 1980s as it tried to destabilize the Marxist government, was among the first to turn to magic; it carved out a special role for witch doctors, whom the Marxists had marginalized. By the time groups in Congo took that technique to its lowest depths in the late 1990s—some child soldiers there were instructed that eating their victims made them stronger—the world started paying attention. Advocates succeeded in placing the child soldier issue on the United Nations agenda and passing protocols that called for the age of combatants to be at least 18 (the United States and Britain are among the countries that have refused to sign). But renegade armed groups continue to be a stumbling block.

Just this month, in a shantytown near Nairobi, Kenya's capital, enforcers from a group called the Mungiki—essentially a street gang that uses teenage muscle—hacked up several opponents in an effort to control the minibus racket. True to form, their leader has told his young henchmen that he rolled to earth in a ball of stars.

Colombian Peace Is Challenged by an Abundance of Child Soldiers

Charles Geisler and Niousha Roshani

In the following viewpoint, Charles Geisler and Niousha Roshani draw a connection between Colombia's high numbers of IDPs (internally displaced persons) and child soldiers. Displaced children are especially vulnerable to being recruited into war because of their poverty. According to the authors, a cycle of displacement-recruitment-displacement is in place in Colombia, and will only cease to exist once the Colombian government takes direct action. Geisler is a professor of development sociology at Cornell University. Roshani is a graduate student in international development at Cornell University.

As you read, consider the following questions:

1. What are the hardships faced by displaced children in Colombia?

2. Why is it difficult to attain an accurate number of IDPs (internally displaced persons) in Colombia?

3. According to the authors, what steps should the government of Colombia take to end the use of child soldiers?

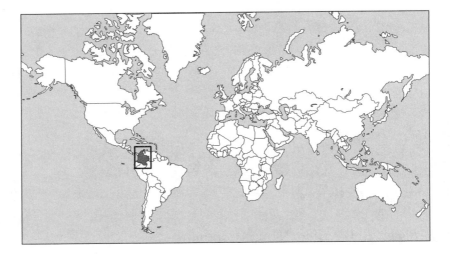

The collateral damage of war falls disproportionately on civilians including children and adolescents. Such damage occurs with high levels of impunity and is quickly forgotten. In countries like Colombia, warfare and its displacing effects have continued for three generations. The children of displaced families are not only the victims of crime and violence, but large numbers are regularly recruited by warring factions as child combatants, thus reproducing and prolonging hostilities. Those committed to peace accords in Colombia face a grim reality: Abundant supplies of adolescent soldiers may postpone peace negotiations indefinitely.

Colombia's population is currently estimated to be 43,700,000, with 16,407,000 under the age of 18. With more than three million reported IDPs [internally displaced persons]—and many more unreported—Colombia has the second highest population of IDPs in the world after the Sudan. The UNDP [United Nations Development Programme] and NGO [nongovernmental organisation] sources believe that youth comprise approximately 50 percent of the internally displaced population. According to Colombia's Consultancy on Human Rights and Displacement (CODHES), 86 percent of all internally displaced people (IDP) households include one or more children. Of these displaced children, 45 percent are 14 or younger, while 20 percent are between 3 and 10 years old.

What Displacement Means for Children

Displacement usually means a series of calamities—homelessness, physical torture, severe trauma and exposure to atrocities, malnutrition, little formal education, loss of family members, and risks of many kinds including constant and recurring military recruitment. For many children without parents, joining a fighting force is a matter of survival. It renders the distinction between forced and voluntary recruitment academic.

It is estimated that 14,000 to 20,000 children are serving in the armed forces in Colombia, placing Colombia fourth in the world for reliance on child soldiers, following Myanmar, Liberia and the Democratic Republic of the Congo. According to Human Rights Watch, at least one of every four irregular combatants in Colombia's civil war is under eighteen years old.

"For many children without parents, joining a fighting force is a matter of survival."

As in many countries, the government of Colombia seldom provides IDP children in flight with special programs or security measures. However, some attention by both national and international organizations is geared towards former child soldiers and their rehabilitation back into society. Absent this, such combatants are faced with physical and sexual abuse, exploitation and abduction, trafficking and renewed recruitment, especially when separated from their families and support networks. Nongovernmental organisations are active in treating children for malnutrition and disease, but rarely do more. Child soldiers seeking to exit military livelihoods often face community lasting distrust and scorn in the local civil environments to which they might flee.

Societal Effects of Child Soldiering

The tragedy of child militias in Colombia and elsewhere then is both personal and societal. Globally, hundreds of thousands of displaced children are catapulted into violent lives that serve adult purposes. Whole societies suffer to the extent that vast "reserve armies" of children perpetuate cultures of war rather than peace, both because of dysfunctional socialization and because incentives to enter peace negotiations are reduced by a virtually unrestrained supply of combatants, regardless of age. Those who lobby for peace must lobby strenuously for an end to internal displacement and the military recruitment of children it spawns.

The mortality rate of Colombia's IDP children may be as high as 120 per 1,000, compared to 21 per 1,000 in this age group for the population as a whole. This former rate may be due to repeated displacements while hiding from armed forces. Conditions of displacement put at risk the entire range of rights guaranteed children by the Convention on the Rights of the Child (CRC), including survival, protection, and development essentials such as education. According to the IDMC [Internal Displacement Monitoring Centre], displaced children may be denied the right to education for lack of proper documentation, inability to pay school fees, racial discrimination, and language barriers among many other factors.

It is difficult to obtain an accurate number of IDPs in Colombia for many reasons. Displaced people of all ages refrain from identifying themselves as displaced for fear of further persecution and discrimination. The guerrilla and paramilitary groups have been known to eliminate IDPs for fear of witnesses providing information on military activities. Registration as a displaced person can also reduce chances of gaining employment or access to education and health services for children. Furthermore, most IDPs come from poor backgrounds in which identification cards are uncommon.

Colombian Society Not Taking Responsibility

How can facts so troubling warrant so little public attention in Colombia? Difficulties in counting IDPs only partially account for why IDP child combatants in Colombia often go largely unnoticed. Colombia is trapped in a displacement-recruitment syndrome. As noted, displacement from armed conflicts begets youth with stark survival choices. According to Human Rights Watch, these adolescents and children are being recruited in growing numbers to fight adult wars, which in turn fuel new rounds of violence and displacement. These intensify the demand for combatants, both young and old. This pernicious cycle has become a way of life in Colombia, invisible in part because it is the norm. Some Colombian children have spent their entire lives as militants and without childhoods.

"Some Colombian children have spent their entire lives as militants and without childhoods."

Many other factors enter this recipe for oblivion. To be sure, few military groups want to advertise that their cause rides on the backs of children. Shame no doubt leads to secrecy as well as denial. Second, as minors, children lack rights to represent themselves. Often they are unaware they have human rights. They are at the mercy of their society and their society is at war. Related to this, child IDPs typically lack identification documents and dwell in social limbo; their disappearance into combat roles easily goes unnoticed, at least officially. Moreover, there is no penalty for such oversight. The government of Colombia can look the other way with impunity and has threatened organizations such as CODHES for purveying negative images of Colombia in the eyes of the national community.

Colombian Children at Risk

- 1.6 million children or youth (under the age of 18) are internally displaced

- 11,000 are child soldiers, of whom 25 percent are girls

- 4,000 children are killed by small arms each year

- 100 are killed each year by land mines

- more than 300 are kidnapped each year

- as many as 35,000 are child prostitutes

- 2.7 million are child labourers

- 30,000 street children are living in dangerous conditions

Canada International Development Agency (CIDA),
"Child Protection: Protecting Children and Youth in Colombia,"
May 13, 2009.

There are other social factors at play. Elite Colombian society often associates IDP children with poverty, misery and other taunts to their national respectability. There is a tendency to blame combatants rather than oligarchs for enduring civil war, in short, blaming the victim, including children. Child combatants inhabit a troubled cultural zone in Colombia no less than their counterparts in other world regions. The lack of census data for such children and more detailed studies of their precarious lives only add to their obscurity and to public disavowals of responsibility.

The Connection Between Child Soldiering and Displacement

But what exactly are the correlations between displacement and child soldiering? What are the consequences, and how might they be prevented? Displacement and child militia are not simply unrelated outcomes of war; they are often deeply interconnected. Whether during war or "peace," there actually appears to be a strong relationship between the risk of recruitment during displacement and the risk of displacement as an outcome of recruitment.

Yet, it seems clear that the most serious risks for children occur in countries in the midst of intense armed conflict, where the numbers of both IDPs and child soldiers often rise. Countries suffering the worst trends in child recruitment, both in numbers and violent treatment, have also tended to produce the largest populations of IDPs and refugees in the world, including literally millions of children.

The disconnect between the IDP status of children and military recruitment is part of a larger syndrome that Colombia and other countries relying on child combatants are experiencing. As displacement spreads, poverty and insecurity spread, and families separate. Children are abducted into or seek out military roles to survive. Military "solutions" to civil difficulties leads to yet more displacement and re-recruitment of child combatants. This is almost surely a lead factor in Human Rights Watch's conclusion last year [2005] that children are being recruited in growing numbers. The displacement-recruitment-displacement cycle has become a way of life in Colombia.

In a rare public comment, Commander Mariana of the FARC-EP's [Fuerzas Armadas Revolucionarias de Colombia—Ejército del Pueblo or "Revolutionary Armed Forces of Colombia—People's Army," a national military-political organization fighting against the Colombian government] Thematic Work Group acknowledged and defended the FARC-EPs' continued recruiting of children: "We do have large numbers of young persons over 15 years of age in our ranks. They dream of a better country for their families, for themselves, and for all those who endure similar conditions. Therefore they made the decision to enlist in the FARC. We even admit, in exceptional cases, persons under that age, because neither the state nor society, nor even their families, are prepared to offer them a chance to lead a decent life. Let's not be shocked at this. Instead, let's look at the options that this society that criticizes us offers them: street begging, joining delinquent gangs in deprived urban districts, resorting to prostitution, joining gangs of paid killers . . . there should be no war . . . unfortunately, those who hold the economic and political power in our country have left the Colombian people no other option than an uprising".

"At least one of every four combatants in Colombia's internal war is a child."

The FARC position is self-justifying. Similar logics may exist within press releases of the Colombian military and paramilitary groups. None would take kindly to our labelling their recruitment of vulnerable populations as predatory. Still, our best estimates suggest that the overall numbers of child soldiers and those that come from the ranks of the displaced remain alarmingly high and do not represent voluntary choice.

Ways to End Child Soldiering in Colombia

There is little doubt that reintegrating displaced children successfully into society—those with and those without military experience—can help reduce the potential for future human rights violations in Colombia and address the psychological, health, economic, and educational needs of vulnerable segment of the population. We suggest further benefits follow from reintegration and concerted prevention of child recruitment: an accelerated peace process. Though direct evidence for this claim would take years to assemble, the proposition seems strong on its face. Warring factions in Colombia will treat the resolution of their differences cavalierly if the pipeline of children keeps producing new recruits. At least one of every four combatants in Colombia's internal war is a child. Colombia's reliance on children to turn the wheels of war is in some ways a modern remake of the thirteenth-century Children's Crusade [a "crusade" of children who marched to convert Muslims to Christianity in 1212; while some believe the march occurred, others believe it is fictional]. Orgies of bloodshed and human displacement could be avoided if children were not sacrificed for such causes.

The government of Colombia could take proactive steps—and win significant support for its position in the civil war—were it to acknowledge the problem and renounce any further recruitment of children soldiers. It should unhesitatingly support nongovernmental organisations, national and other, that have taken up the cause of children soldiers and their social reintegration.

The vicious cycle that has been described here is morally repulsive. It is also a poorly understood obstacle to peacemaking in Colombia's troubled social landscape. Perhaps among the children that are spared military servitude are the future leaders who will, for good reason, never let this tragedy reoccur in Colombia.

The United States Treats Captured Child Soldiers as if They Are Criminals

Vincent J. Curtis

In the following viewpoint, Vincent J. Curtis describes the condi-tions at Guantánamo Bay in Cuba, where Canadian-born Omar Khadr is being held. Khadr was captured at the age of fifteen in Afghanistan after he allegedly threw a grenade that injured and later killed a U.S. marine. Khadr's status is that of detainee rather than prisoner of war, pending the outcome of his trial, which at the time of writing was to be conducted under the au-thority of the Military Commissions Act of 2006. Khadr, twenty-two years old in 2008, is reported to be housed in Guantánamo's Camp IV facility, which appears to have the same design and procedures as a medium-security penitentiary. Curtis expects Khadr to remain living under these conditions until the outcome of his trial is known. Curtis is a journalist for Esprit de Corps.

As you read, consider the following questions:

1. What are two reasons for using the Guantánamo Bay facility to hold those captured in Iraq and Afghanistan?
2. What was Omar Khadr's alleged crime in July 2002?
3. What are the characteristics of trials carried out under the Military Commissions Act of 2006?

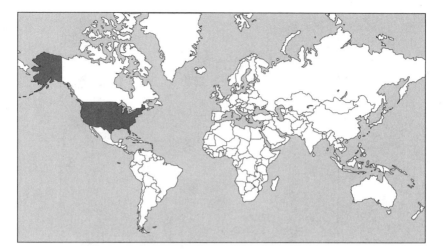

In January 2008, Vincent J. Curtis travelled to the U.S. military prison in Guantánamo Bay, Cuba.

The most famous Canadian on the island of Cuba isn't basking on a beach, sipping rum, or sucking on a huge stogie. The most famous Canadian in Cuba has never enjoyed a languorous anti-American tirade with Fidel Castro, the retired Cuban president. The most famous Canadian in Cuba resides in Camp Delta, Naval Station Guantánamo, an unhappy guest of the United States government. His name is Omar Khadr.

Guantánamo Bay is situated on the southeast coast of Cuba. The bay is shaped like a bent figure eight. The southern, outer harbor is open to the Caribbean Sea, and it and the land around it are leased by the United States from Cuba under a treaty first negotiated in 1903. The inner harbor, the top of the figure eight, remains entirely in Cuban hands.

Gitmo [Guantánamo Bay] began as a coaling station for the American fleet that protected the Panama Canal; and the last of its major missions decamped for the continental United States in the middle 1990s. The naval station was used as a place to house refugees fleeing the chaos of Haiti, but by the turn of the millennium the only thing going on at the base was keeping the lights burning.

Underage Prisoners Detained at Guantánamo

Name	Date of Birth	In-Processing Date	In-Processing Age
Abdul Qudus	DD MMM 88	07 FEB 02	13–14
Assad Ullah	DD MMM 88	23 MAR 03	14–15
Naqib Ullah	DD MMM 88	07 FEB 03	14–15
Mohammed Omar	DD MMM 86	12 JUN 02	15–16
Muhammed Hamid Al Qarani	DD MMM 86	09 FEB 02	15–16
Shams Ullah	DD MMM 86	28 OCT 02	15–16
Omar Ahmed Khadr	19 SEPT 86	28 OCT 02	16
Yussef Mohammed Mubarak Al Shihri	08 SEPT 85	16 JAN 02	16
Mohamed Jawad	DD MMM 85	18 DEC 02	16–17
Yasser Talal Al Zahrani	22 SEPT 84	21 JAN 02	17
Abdul Salam Ghetan	14 DEC 84	17 JAN 02	17

TAKEN FROM: "Guantánamo's Children: Military and Diplomatic Testimonies," Center for the Study of Human Rights in the Americas (UC-Davis), November 3, 2008. http://humanrights.ucdavis.edu/.

The attacks on 9/11 changed all that. The collapse of the Taliban regime in Afghanistan produced a flood of captives, and some of the flow was hustled into captivity by Canada's JTF2 [Joint Task Force 2] commandos working in cooperation with the U.S. military. A secure place was needed to incarcerate the al Qaeda and Taliban captives, and the facilities of Gitmo were pressed into service.

Gitmo was chosen for a variety of reasons. First, it is remarkably secure. No one can get in or out except by air or sea. No one can land in Gitmo without permission. The U.S. Coast Guard patrols the waters approaching it. There are no innocent civilians who can get caught in a cross fire should terrorists make an attempt against the base.

A more important reason perhaps was the unique legal status of NS-GTMO. Gitmo is sovereign Cuban territory, and a Canadian national living in Cuba does not obviously come under the jurisdiction of a civilian U.S. court, or enjoy the rights enumerated in the U.S. Constitution. That hasn't stopped American lawyers from trying to get civilian U.S. courts to intervene on behalf of their clients, but the severely restricted access to the base has kept the so-called "Habeas" lawyers from turning Gitmo into a circus. Khadr's case itself has received a spirited defence from the military lawyer assigned to him, Lt.-Cmdr. William Kuebler.

Khadr (or "Carter" as his name is pronounced by the Americans at Gitmo) is considered to be a potential war criminal, and is classed as an "unlawful alien enemy combatant" under the Military Commissions Act of 2006. On the property of the naval station is Camp Delta, which, in turn, contains all the camps used for the detention operations. Within the confines of Delta are Camps I through VI, which hold or once held detainees. There is also Camp America, which houses the guard force. Khadr was last reported to be held in Camp IV, which is like a medium-security penitentiary. The perimeter of Delta is heavily guarded, and photographs of the beach defenses are not allowed.

Khadr is referred to as a detainee rather than a POW. By presidential order of February 2002, no civilian captured in Afghanistan is deemed to be a prisoner of war as that term is defined in the Third Geneva Convention of 1949. Detainee is a term that holds Khadr's Geneva status in suspense, pending the outcome of his trial.

"Khadr (or 'Carter' as his name is pronounced by the Americans at Gitmo) is considered to be a potential war criminal, and is classed as an 'unlawful alien enemy combatant' under the Military Commissions Act of 2006."

Khadr is accused of killing SFC Christopher J. Speer while dressed as a civilian during a battle in Afghanistan. Khadr himself was severely wounded in that battle. If convicted, his status would change from detainee to prisoner, but that change in status would not affect his day-to-day routine in the camp. Even if he were found innocent of any crime, he would not be automatically released from Gitmo.

Khadr's trial is being conducted under the authority of the Military Commissions Act of 2006, an act of the U.S. Congress which authorizes the United States military to hold "commissions" (proceedings styled after a court-martial). The maximum penalties under the act are death or life imprisonment; lesser punishment is also possible. Khadr's trial, among the first of the commissions, has so far been bogged down with preliminary defense motions. Khadr's trial, and most of the other commissions, will take place in Camp Justice, which lies on a disused airfield outside Delta, and was constructed especially for the commissions.

Camp IV is designed like a medium-security penitentiary, and appears to operate with similar procedures. The detainees in Camp IV live communally in barrack blocks that hold up to ten each. The camp can accommodate up to 100 detainees. Detainees are allowed up to 12 hours per day for recreation, and there is a soccer pitch in the middle of the recreation yard. Inmates can receive instruction on reading and writing in English and Arabic if they wish, and have access to a 6,000-item library. They can also watch an HDTV in the classroom. An arrow pointing in the direction of Mecca is painted on the floor of every room in the Camp. Detainees are kept informed of world events through a newsletter that is posted weekly in the recreation yard. What the detainees are allowed to possess is strictly controlled.

To date, the Canadian government has made no diplomatic effort to claim jurisdiction over Khadr, or to have him transferred to Canadian custody. That may change once the outcome of his commission trial is known. Until then he will have to sit and wait as the most famous Canadian in Cuba.

Young Girls Are Soldiers, Too

Susan McKay

In the following viewpoint, Susan McKay points out that girls also are child soldiers and that they face unique horrors while in combat. Girls play a number of roles in fighting forces including preparing food, carrying and/or using weapons, and providing health services, but they also are forced to provide sexual services to men and boy soldiers. The trauma of being sexually abused goes well beyond the moment and affects these girls throughout their lives. McKay is a professor of women's studies at the Uni-versity of Wyoming. She also co-wrote Where Are the Girls? Girls in Fighting Forces in Northern Uganda, Sierra Leone, and Mozambique: Their Lives During and After War.

As you read, consider the following questions:

1. According to Susan McKay, what are some of the reasons girls join fighting forces?
2. While in fighting forces, why, according to the author, must girls sometimes develop their friendships in secrecy?

3. What does it mean to be a "rebel wife" or a "rebel baby"?

Most people are surprised to learn that girls are widely used as child soldiers. . . . Between the years 1990 and 2003, girls were present in fighting forces (government forces, paramilitary/militia, and armed opposition groups) in fifty-five countries; in thirty-eight of these countries they were involved in situations of armed conflict. How do they enter these forces? Like boys, some girls join with their families and friends—because of family expectations, for ideological reasons, and/or in response to state violence. Others become part of fighting forces to escape physical and psychological abuse and sexual violence at home; because they perceive that they have few or no choices about their own futures; and/or to seek lives at variance with traditional societal expectations. They may join to gain education and improve career opportunities, and/or because they imagine they will find greater gender equality such as occurred widely in Peru when an estimated 40 percent of guerrillas in the Shining Path were female. Many were girls or college students when they joined, recruited by their professors. The notion of girls freely joining, however, is a contested one, because these girls usually lack quality choices.

Children may be taken as orphans, as in Sri Lanka, or be born into a force. Many girls and boys are abducted or otherwise forced to join. Between 1990 and 2003, girls were abducted into armed forces and groups in eleven countries in Africa, four in the Americas, eight in Asia, three in Europe, and two in the Middle East. Many abducted children are also transported across international borders, especially in Africa. In a study of forty Sierra Leonean girls, it was discovered that all were abducted by the Revolutionary United Front (RUF). They reported extreme coercion, violence, and fear, usually under the threat of a gun, and being forcibly separated from loved ones.

The Abuse of Girl Soldiers

Girls' roles typically overlap and include working as spies and informants, in intelligence and communications, and as military trainers and combatants. They are health workers and mine sweepers, and they conduct suicide missions. Other support roles include raising crops, selling goods, preparing food, carrying loot and weapons, and stealing food, livestock, and seed stock. Important to understand is that underlying these various roles and activities, girls' participation is central to sustaining a force because of their productive and reproductive labor. As such, they replicate traditional societal gender roles and patriarchal privilege, whereby girls (and women) serve men and boys. Their labor is a foundation upon which fighting forces throughout the world rely.

Girls in fighting forces, especially when they have been abducted, often experience physical and psychological abuse including sexual violence—although its occurrence varies by context, because some fighting forces eschew forced sex. Between 1990 and 2003, girls provided sexual services to boys and men in fighting forces in nine African countries, three countries in the Americas, five in Asia, and two in Europe. Again, depending on the context, when they reach puberty, girls may supply reproductive labor by giving birth to and rearing children who will become members of the force. For example, in the Lord's Resistance Army (LRA) fighting force in Northern Uganda, the leader, Joseph Kony, has fathered large numbers of children, who have grown up in his force. Girls in fighting forces in Mozambique, Northern Uganda, and Sierra Leone reported sexual violence, and abducted girls were almost universally raped—often by many men during a single day. As in Sierra Leone, sex labor was integral to the function of girl soldiers in Angola. In contrast, within forces in Colombia, Sri Lanka, and the Philippines, sexual violence toward girl combatants in rebel forces is not common.

As yet, we know little about distinctions between girls and women in terms of psychological effects of sexual violence and how identity and self-esteem may be affected, although lifelong effects can be expected. We do know that throughout the world girls (and women) are stigmatized and marginalized when they experience sexual violence. Girls feel shame, and their communities may consider them to be morally compromised and not marriageable. With their bodies still developing, girls who are subjected to repeated sexual violence experience genital damage such as vaginal lacerations, which in turn make them more vulnerable to STDs. Sterility may also result. Although most data are anecdotal because of a lack of systematic epidemiologic studies, many girls purportedly die during pregnancy and childbirth because of immature bodies, unsafe conditions, and lack of health care.

"Throughout the world girls (and women) are stigmatized and marginalized when they experience sexual violence."

How Girl Soldiers' Experiences Affect Their Lives

It is important to reiterate that within fighting forces, girls' experiences are multifaceted, complex, and context specific. Thus, a girl soldier in a Colombian rebel force may have distinctly different experiences from a girl in Angola or Indonesia. Yet, they share commonalities such as altered identity and changed human networks, behaviors, and relationships. Physically, they are challenged to survive as they cope with illnesses, exhaustion, wounds, menstrual difficulties, complications from pregnancy and birth, STDs, and a host of other maladies such as malaria, intestinal parasites, tuberculosis, anemia, diarrhea, malnutrition, disabilities, scars, and burns.

Exposed daily to a culture of violence and themselves perpetrators in acts of terror such as attacking their own families and neighbors, abducting other children, and killing civilians, they are no longer normal girls either in their own eyes or in the eyes of those who know them. Instead, girlhood is inverted and distorted. They have experienced what most of us never imagine, and they can never go back to girlhood innocence. Relationships and networks also are altered drastically. For girls, being apart from their mothers is one of their greatest hardships. They may also be forbidden to spend time with other girls because they might conspire to escape. Consequently, friendships may develop in secrecy. In Angola, some girls reported solidarity and friendship with other girls. Similarly, in Sierra Leone girls formed close relationships with other girls and women, which reduced their fear and brought solace, comfort, and solidarity. Also, older women sometimes offered protection to them.

"They are no longer normal girls either in their own eyes or in the eyes of those who know them."

Although still limited, we now have greater understanding about how girls' experiences change them psychologically and how identities may or may not be transformed within fighting forces. For example, some young girls who were abducted into the RUF but only stayed a short time were not subjected to sexual violence and were welcomed home; their identities appeared to remain reasonably intact. In contrast, during the forty-year war in Angola, girls in the forces underwent deliberate suppression of their identities that resulted in diminished memories of relationships, place, and community. Their constant movement from place to place across the countryside led to their losing a sense of time, sequencing of events, and parts of their own identity. Such girls may find it difficult to recall their ages or how long they were in a force, or to retain identities that link them with civilian life.

Percentage of Boys and Girls of All Children Involved in Armed Conflict Worldwide

Total number of children involved in armed conflict, worldwide, is estimated at 300,000

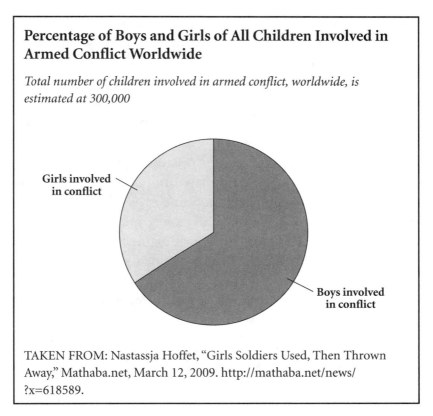

Girls involved in conflict

Boys involved in conflict

TAKEN FROM: Nastassja Hoffet, "Girls Soldiers Used, Then Thrown Away," Mathaba.net, March 12, 2009. http://mathaba.net/news/?x=618589.

Changes in Girls' Identity

Other girls have profound transformations in their identities because they become mothers, often from forced sex. They no longer view themselves as girls—despite their chronological age—because girlhood may be perceived to end when marriage and motherhood begin, as is true in many cultures. Because we presently know little about these mothers, critical questions remain to be asked, for example: In societies where being unmarried is tantamount to social exclusion, and marriage and motherhood convey womanhood, how do girls negotiate identity when they return with children fathered by unidentifiable males? What does it mean to a girl's identity when she returns from a fighting force and is called a "rebel wife" and her baby a "rebel baby," born of an unsanctioned marriage?

Another identity change that can occur for girls is developing a sense of self as efficacious [having the power to affect something]. Many girls brutalized by violence found their identities changed, often gradually, from being victims of violence to perpetrators. Although most Sierra Leonean girl soldiers were abducted and subjected to continual violence, over time some girls gained power. For example, some girl soldiers in Sierra Leone were empowered because they resisted sexual violence, rebelled against authority and command structure and participated in violent acts. Some girls who carried and used light weapons felt a sense of power and control, which, at the time, they relished. Other girls aligned themselves with commanders as "wives" and thereby gained protection, power, and status.

Notably, however, many—probably most—girls are not empowered because they are not fighters, do not possess weapons, or are not privileged by their position within a force. In Angola, for example, of a group of forty girl soldiers only three reported that they worked as soldiers per se, whereas the rest worked in logistics and support. As observed by child psychiatrist Elizabeth Jareg, a program adviser to Save the Children Norway:

> Many [girls] experience frontline service and not infrequently express satisfaction that for the first time in their lives they have power and an equal status with men. Others have years-long experiences of being continually abused and forced to bear children with men who treat them brutally.

Therefore, recognizing how varied girls' experiences are is critical to better understanding how identity may be shaped in fighting forces. Similarly, we can expect that in the post-conflict aftermath girls' identities will vary according to age when enlisted, length of time in a force, experiences, and roles.

Periodical Bibliography

America	"Peace in Northern Uganda?" April 16, 2007.
Jo Becker	"Child Soldiers: Changing a Culture of Violence," *Human Rights*, Winter 2005.
Christian Caryl	"Iraq's Young Blood," *Newsweek*, January 22, 2007.
Nadja Drost	"Postcard from Medellín," *TIME*, April 23, 2009.
Jeffrey Gettleman	"Armed & Underage: Across the Globe, Thousands of Children Are Being Forced to Serve as Soldiers," *New York Times Upfront*, April 20, 2009.
Jeffrey Gettleman	"The Perfect Weapon: Thousands of Child Soldiers Have Been Forced into Battle in Some of Africa's Most Violent Conflicts," *New York Times Upfront*, September 3, 2007.
Tom Masland	"BOOKS: Killing Off Innocence; Why Children Serve in Three Fourths of Armed Conflicts," *Newsweek*, February 14, 2005.
MWC News	"Pakistan 'Rescues' Child Soldiers," July 29, 2009. http://mwcnews.net.
National Review	"In the Bloodstained History of Terrorism, the Tamil Tigers Will Always Have a Place, Alongside the IRA, the Taliban, the Chechens, and the PLO," June 8, 2009.
Alissa Quart	"The Child Soldiers of Staten Island: While Hollywood Swoons over Teen Guerillas, the Real Lost Boys Are Hidden in Plain Sight," *Mother Jones*, July-August 2007.
P.W. Singer	"Children at War," *Military History*, September 2007.
Tim Stafford	"A New Kind of War," *Books & Culture*, November-December 2007.

GLOBALVIEWPOINTS

CHAPTER 2

The Causes and Effects of Children in Combat

Threats and Promises Entice Children to War

P.W. Singer

In the following viewpoint, P.W. Singer outlines the ways in which children are coerced, or forced, into soldiering. Singer points out that choices are not freely made for those children who "volunteer" for war. Children are different than adults in their capacity to make mature decisions, and Singer argues that adults need to prevent children from entering war. Additionally, many children are drawn to war because of their backgrounds of poverty and violence. Singer is senior fellow and director of the 21st Century Defense Initiative at the Brookings Institution. He also wrote Wired for War.

As you read, consider the following questions:

1. According to the author, what is the main standard used to determine whether a child is physically capable of soldiering?

2. Which groups of children are at particular risk for recruitment into war?

3. According to the author, how can a child's economic situation factor into his/her decision to join armed groups?

Transforming a child into a fairly effective combatant is disturbingly simple. It begins with recruitment, either through abduction or "voluntary" means. Recruitment is rapidly followed by cruel but straightforward methods of training and conversion. Brutality and abuses of the worst kind underscore each stage, but these lie in part behind the overall program's usual effectiveness. The ultimate aim of the process is to foster a child's dependency on an armed organization and inhibit escape.

Case studies indicate that in the majority of conflicts, a primary method of recruitment of children is through some form of abduction. Typically, recruiting parties are given conscription targets that change according to the group's need and objective. For example, the UPC/RP [Union des Patriotes Congolais/Reconcialition et Paix], a militia led by Thomas Lubanga in the eastern Congo, has a policy that each family within its area of control must provide a cow, money, or child to the group. Often, the groups develop practices that are quite efficient. For example, the LRA [Lord's Resistance Army, Ugandan rebel group] sets numeric goals for child recruits and sends raiding parties into villages to meet them. Other groups, such as the LTTE [Liberation Tigers of Tamil Eelam, Sri Lanka], reportedly maintain sophisticated computerized population databases to direct their recruiting efforts.

"The ultimate aim [of transforming a child into a soldier] is to foster a child's dependency on an armed organization and inhibit escape."

All children are not automatically taken in such operations, but only those who meet certain criteria decided by the groups' leaders. The main standard is physical size, with the ability to bear a weapon being the normal cutoff point. Literally, recruiters will place a weapon in the child's hands to see if he or she is yet strong enough to hold it. Other groups use alternative proxies to measure physical development. The SPLA [Sudan People's Liberation Army], for instance, uses the presence of two molar teeth to determine whether the child is ready to serve.

Child Recruitment

These standards not only illustrate the young ages often pulled in, but also how child recruitment is often a meticulously planned process. Those children who are judged too small to carry weapons or looted goods will either be set free or killed in order to intimidate both the local populace and the new recruits. Similarly, if the plan is to seize girls as attendants to more senior members of the group, only those considered more attractive might be taken. These goals are taken quite seriously, and failure to meet them risks punishment from superiors.

The decision of where groups carry out their operations to find their recruits is also based on planned efforts to maximize the efficiency of their efforts. Both state armies and rebel groups typically target the places where children will both be collected in the greatest number and are most vulnerable to being swept in. These range from stadiums and buses to mosques and churches.

The most frequent targets are secondary schools or orphanages, where children of suitable size are collected in one place, but out of contact with their parents, who would try to spirit them away. Indeed, the LTTE even took to setting up a unit formed exclusively of orphans, the elite Sirasu Puli (Leopard Brigade). The Congolese Rally for Democracy-Goma (RCD-Goma) and Rwandan Patriotic Army (RPA) are two other groups that also target schools almost exclusively, using kidnapping or coercion to pull in kids. Another common target area is the marketplace. For instance, during the Ethiopian fighting in the 1990s, a common practice was that armed militias would simply surround the public bazaar. They would

order every male to sit down and then force into a truck any-
one deemed "eligible." This often included minors.

Homeless or street children are at particular risk, as they
are most vulnerable to sweeps aimed at them, which prompt
less public outcry. In Sudan, for instance, the government set
up camps for street children, and then rounded up children to
fill them in a purported attempt to "clean up" Khartoum.
These camps, however, served as reservoirs for army conscription.

Other groups that are at frequent danger are refugee and
IDP (internally displaced persons) populations. In many instances, families on the run become disconnected. Armed
groups then target unaccompanied, and thus more vulnerable,
minors.

---

*"The most frequent targets are secondary schools or or-
phanages, where children of suitable size are collected in
one place, but out of contact with their parents."*

Failing to Provide Protection

The international community can even become unintention-
ally complicit in the recruitment of children, if it is not careful in its own practices. For example, in the Sudanese civil
war, unaccompanied minors living in the UNHCR [United
Nations High Commissioner for Refugees] refugee camps
were housed in separate areas from the rest of the refugee
population. As the camps had no security, the SPLA easily targeted the boys. Indeed, certain rebel commanders even sought
to have camps placed near them, not for humanitarian reasons, but so that they could maintain a reserve of recruits
close at hand.

I was abducted during "Operation Pay Yourself," in 1998. I
was 9 years old. Six rebels came through our yard. They
went to loot for food. It's called "jaja"—"get food." They

said, "We want to bring a small boy like you—we like you." My mother didn't comment; she just cried. My father objected. They threatened to kill him. They argued with him at the back of the house. I heard a gunshot. One of them told me, "Let's go, they've killed your father." A woman rebel grabbed my hand roughly and took me along. I saw my father lying dead as we passed.

—A., age fourteen

Even national borders can fail to provide protection. In numerous instances, rebel groups target foreign villages just across the borders, which heretofore might have been considered outside the danger zone. In the Liberian war, for example, it was not uncommon to come across a child from Sierra Leone who had been abducted into the fighting. Similar cases hold in the Myanmar war with Thailand, the Colombian war with Peru, and all the nations surrounding the Democratic Republic of the Congo (DRC).

The New Genocide

In many ways, these tactics of abduction and impressment into service echo the naval press gangs of the Napoleonic era. The difference is not just the lower ages, however. Present-day abduction raids are not only about building one's force, but are also instruments of war in and of themselves. Forced recruitment of children is often just one aspect in a larger campaign carried out by an armed group, designed to intimidate local civilian communities. Having already crossed one line of propriety, armed groups that abduct children for soldiering are also inclined to go on rape and looting rampages while in the villages. Likewise, the children of certain ethnic groups might be targeted, in particular if there is a chance to use child soldiers against their co-ethnics on the other side. This was the case in Guatemala, where government recruitment of minors usually focused on the children of ethnic groups that had been in the political opposition. The indigenous Mayans called the theft of their young "the new genocide."

It was an unbelievable and unreal event when the rebels arrested me and my family. We were told to carry their loads on our heads. We did so for some time and my sister cried out in pain to tell them she was sick and wanted to rest. The rebels asked us if we all wanted to rest, not knowing that after telling them we wanted to rest, they had planned something else for us.

We were left seated there for a while and they came back with cutlasses [machetes] and a log of wood. We knew too well what these things mean, because we have heard that with these things they cut off the hands and feet of people. Now we were in a hideous state—they killed my parents in front of me, my uncle's hands were cut off and my sister was raped in front of us by their commander called "Spare No Soul." After all this happened, they told us, the younger boys, to join them. If not, they were going to kill us. I was in place to die with my parents because I felt like killing them myself—but they had something which I did not: a gun. I and my sister were left in a traumatized state. We had no parents any longer, and my sister was in pain after having been raped, and my own toe was cut off.

—R., age unknown

For those children who are forcibly taken, it is often "a journey into hell." Abduction is by definition an act of violence that rips terrified children from the security of their families and homes. Killings, rapes, and severe beatings often accompany it. Once caught, children have no choice; usually they must comply with their captors or die.

A Less than "Voluntary" Recruitment

Not all children are forced into soldiering, though. Many may choose to join an armed group of their own volition and thus the groups that use them often claim they broke no moral codes. The rough trend line seems to be that roughly two of every three child soldiers have some sort of initiative in their own recruitment. For example, estimates are that 40 percent of the FARC's [Revolutionary Armed Forces of Colobmia's] child soldiers are forced into service, and 60 percent joined of their own volition. Another survey in East Asia found that 57 percent of the children had volunteered. Finally, a survey of child soldiers in four African countries found that 64 percent joined under no threat of violence.

To describe this choice as voluntary, however, is greatly misleading. Children are defined as such, not only because of their lesser physical development, but also because they are judged to be of an age at which they are not capable of making mature decisions. By contrast, to go to war and risk one's life in an act that has societal-wide consequences is one of the most serious decisions a person can make. This is why the previous four thousand years of leaders left this choice to mature adults.

> But how can a child volunteer? Because if I volunteer, maybe I don't know what I am doing, but you, the grown-up, should know. And you should stop me from volunteering being a soldier. It wasn't my choice. It wasn't the choice I had to become a soldier.
>
> —C., child soldier from age nine to fifteen

The most basic reason that children join armed groups is that they are driven to do so by forces beyond their control. A particularly strong factor is economic. Hunger and poverty are endemic in conflict zones. Children, particularly those orphaned or disconnected from civil society, may volunteer to join any group if they believe that this is the only way to guarantee regular meals, clothing, or medical attention. As one young boy in the DRC explained, "I joined [President Laurent-Désiré] Kabila's army when I was 13 because my home had been looted and my parents were gone. As I was then on my own, I decided to become a soldier." Indeed, surveys of demobilized child soldiers in the DRC found that almost 60 percent originally joined armed groups because of simple poverty. The same ratio was found in a separate survey of child soldiers half the globe away in East Asia, indicating a broader international trend.

> The military was in need of people to increase their number. All the boys in the village were asked to join the army. There was no way out. If I left the village I would get killed by the rebels who would think that I was a spy. On the other hand, if I stayed in the village and refused to join the army, I wouldn't be given food and would eventually be thrown out, which was as good as being dead.
>
> —*I., age fourteen*

Few Choices

There are no hard-and-fast rules. However, poorer children are typically more vulnerable to being pulled into conflict and are overrepresented in child soldier groups. Not only is their desperation typically higher, but also there is a higher correlation between family dysfunction (an additional driving force) and lower socioeconomic status.

To be fully understood, these decisions must therefore be read within the environment in which they take place. In Afghanistan, for instance, boys growing up over the last decades are likely to have never known running water or electricity, and many will have lost one or more parents to the fighting. By the age of ten, most forgo school and are simply trying to find a way to support themselves. One report tellingly illustrated how a set of Afghan boys were so desperate that they literally had to choose between following a cow around to scoop up its excrement to sell as fuel or joining one of the armed factions. The choice of war may be more dangerous, but it at least provides free clothes, food, and some modicum of respect. Or, as one Congolese child soldier similarly described, "I heard that the rebels at least were eating. So, I joined them."

The same factors may also drive parents to offer their children for combat service when they cannot provide for them on their own. In some cases, armies pay a minor soldier's wages directly to the family. Other case studies tell of parents who encourage their daughters to become soldiers if their marriage prospects are poor. As one study done in Sierra Leone described, "Many mothers have remarked on the joy of seeing their ten-year-old dressed in a brand-new military attire carrying an AK-47. For some families the looted property that child soldiers brought home further convinced them of the need to send more children to the war front to augment scarce income."

"A set of Afghan boys were so desperate that they literally had to choose between following a cow around to scoop up its excrement to sell as fuel or joining one of the armed factions."

More perniciously, some parents may see material advantages in their children's death. In Sri Lanka, parents within LTTE-controlled zones who lose a child are treated with special status as "great hero families." They pay no taxes, receive job preferences, and are allocated special seats at all public events. This type of familial prompting toward children's participation in terrorism and the cult of martyrdom has been a great concern in the Israeli-Palestinian violence. . . . Parents may also drive children into war indirectly. A good portion of girl soldiers who join as "volunteers" cite domestic abuse or exploitation as the underlying reason.

Early Trauma Leads Children to War

Structural conditions in the midst of conflict may also oblige children to join armed organizations for their own protection. Surrounded by violence and chaos, children may decide they are safer in a conflict group, with guns in their own hands,

---

Volunteering Under Threat

"They gave me a uniform and told me that now I was in the army. They even gave me a new name: 'Pisco.' They said that they would come back and kill my parents if I didn't do as they said." Report of interview with a 17-year-old former child soldier in 2006.

"Voices of Child Soldiers," Child Soldiers, December 13, 2007.

---

than going about by themselves unarmed. In one survey of child soldiers in Africa, nearly 80 percent had witnessed combat around their home, 70 percent had their family home destroyed, and just over 59 percent had a family member become a casualty of war. As one child in Liberia (whose nickname was "Colonel One More War") noted of why he joined an armed faction, "We can't sit out. People are killing some of our friends. Can't die for nothing, so I took gun and fight. Thanks God I survived."

Many children may have personally experienced or been witness to the furthest extremes of violence including massacres, summary executions, ethnic cleansing, death squad killings, bombings, torture, sexual abuse, and destruction of home or property. Thus, vengeance can also be a particularly powerful impetus to join the conflict.

Often, child soldiers are the survivors of family massacres. They experience what is known as "survivor's guilt," and are often filled with anger and desire for revenge. Indeed, a number of child soldiers are motivated to join warring factions by the seemingly noble belief that they are helping to prevent other children from losing their parents. Only afterwards do they reflect that they may end up creating the same cycle for other children.

However, such victimization need not always be directly personal for the child to feel its power. The violence may have happened to a family member, a friend, a neighbor, or even some member of a group that the child feels a part of and thus experiences the incident almost as deeply.

> My father, mother, and brothers were killed by the enemy, I became angry. I didn't have any other way to do, unless I have to revenge. And to revenge is only to have a gun. If I have a gun I can revenge. I can fight and avenge my mother, father and brothers. That is the decision I took to become a soldier. The day my mother and father and brothers were killed, the enemy came by surprise. They attacked the village, they gathered the people and after that they took all the cows, and they burned all the houses, even all our clothes were burned inside the houses. We remained naked, without food, and we were suffering, from hunger even. Nakedness was also a problem. Then I decided what to do. I thought I'd better join the army [SPLA].

> —M., age sixteen

Democratic Republic of the Congo's Forgotten Children of Conflict

Anushka Asthana

In the following viewpoint, Anushka Asthana argues that although rehabilitating former child soldiers in the Democratic Republic of the Congo (DRC) is challenging, it is both possible and necessary. Rehabilitating these children is difficult because they have been both the recipients and the source of extreme violence including mutilation and rape. In the most extreme sense, their childhoods have been taken away. Asthana points out that although the war in the DRC has been over for two years, the violence continues, and former child soldiers continue to be turned away by their families and communities. Asthana is a journalist for the Guardian.

As you read, consider the following questions:

1. Why did 15-year-old Emmanuele reportedly join the rebel army group in the Democratic Republic of the Congo?

2. Approximately how many child soldiers are there in the Democratic Republic of the Congo?

3. What is the "resource curse" of the Democratic Republic of the Congo as described in the article?

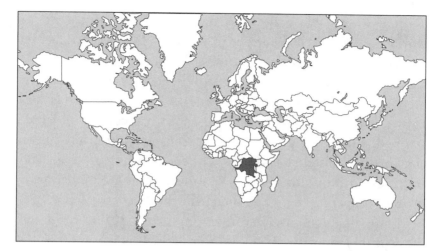

'They made me kill.' Emmanuele looked at the ground as he fumbled with the tassels on his coat. 'If I refused to go to the front line they beat me. They treated me like an animal.'

Emmanuele was 15 when he joined a rebel army group in the Democratic Republic of Congo. The decision was his own. 'I had no money and they said they would give me some,' he said. Other children were taken by force. Serge was at school when a group arrived, firing shots in the air and setting fire to the building. 'I was afraid but I had to go.' He was taken to an army base in Bunia, in the largest town in the Ituri region of the country, where he was put to work on a roadblock.

Serge was then eight. 'I remember holding a gun and shooting,' he said, dropping his voice. 'When it stopped all I could see was bodies on the ground. I knew it must be me who had killed them.' Racked by guilt and missing home Serge cried all the time. He desperately wanted to leave but did not know how.

Eventually he was released and taken to a Save the Children camp in the city of Goma, where he now waits to be reunited with his parents.

It has been two years since the conflict, known as Africa's world war, was officially declared over, but the violence has yet to stop. So far it has claimed more than three million lives.

While hostility has undoubtedly lessened, militias associated with various groups continue to roam the forests and towns. Over the years they have raped, murdered and kidnapped. Boys and girls, still in primary school, have been snatched to bolster their forces. Others as young as seven volunteered to join either the government militia or rebel army groups, desperate to escape their wretched poverty.

Emmanuele and Serge are among about 30,000 child soldiers in the country, 12,500 of them girls. It is common to see children in camouflage uniforms on the roads, with one—or several—weapons slung across their shoulders.

"It is common to see children in camouflage uniforms on the roads, with . . . weapons slung across their shoulders."

The plight of these forgotten children of conflict will be thrust into the public consciousness again by Bob Geldof's Live 8 concerts and when thousands demonstrate at the G8 summit in Scotland next month. Long-term aid to help these children return to their communities and rebuild their lives will be among their demands.

Indeed, the report of the Commission for Africa, signed by Geldof, Tony Blair and Gordon Brown among others, has already highlighted the fact that in African conflicts it is women and children who suffer most, 'recruited—often by force—as combatants, porters or "wives" for male combatants.'

And in the Democratic Republic of Congo groups such as Save the Children and the United Nations children's agency UNICEF have been informally trying to release child fighters since 1999.

After the establishment of a transitional government in 2003 these efforts became increasingly coordinated. A year ago a national programme for Disarmament, Demobilisation and Reinsertion (DDR) was adopted and thousands of children began to return home. During the past 12 months, Save the Children has demobilised 2,500 child soldiers. UNICEF has helped nearly 3,000.

In Goma, by the border with Rwanda, six girls aged between 13 and 17 were sitting on rotting mattresses. Aimerance, 17, wore a lacy top, her long hair in a ponytail. She was breast-feeding her son. Next to her, 13-year-old Furaa was holding her newborn daughter.

All six had been taken from army groups where each had fought on the front line. 'If I refused to fight they beat me,' said Zoe, 17. Zaina, also 17, added: 'When I made a mistake or shot a bullet for no reason, I was whipped with a rope with a knot in it.' Each girl had a different reason for joining up. Zaina said she fled her family home after her father found out she had had sex. 'I thought he would kill me,' she said.

Vumilla went after the war left her an orphan. The others talked about the promise of food and clothes, things that were scarce at home. 'In the army they gave us body oil, clothes and money,' said Zaina. 'We don't get that now.'

Penninah Mathenge, a Save the Children health manager based in the eastern Masisi region, said it was common for poverty to drive children to take up arms. 'When they join the army they are given $15, food and a uniform,' she said.

The country is one of the richest in the world for natural resources, packed with copper, gold and diamonds. Next to the jagged roads, the beautiful Congolese countryside is awash with lush growth, a patchwork quilt of brown and green fields crammed with millet, bean plants and banana palms.

Yet child after child talked about how hunger and desperation led them to become soldiers. It is a poverty that perversely is being driven by the country's natural wealth. Instead of being used to feed and clothe the population, it is traded for arms by the militias which recruit the child soldiers. Most of the wealth is exported to countries across the world, including Britain.

This process is made possible by corruption. 'We call it the resource curse,' said Patrick Alley, director of the Global Witness campaign group. 'Through colonial times and up to today the Congo has been a repository for resources, with no one giving a damn about the people.'

In a graphic demonstration of this, another group, Human Rights Watch, reported last week that gold in the north-east of the country was fuelling atrocities, with armed groups using its profits to fund their activities and buy weapons. This lure of resources together with ethnic divisions have combined to cause the world's worst humanitarian crisis.

"Reintegrating the children into normal life is difficult. Some people find it hard to accept the return of a girl who has been raped."

And as well as driving millions of people into ever deeper poverty and turning children into killers, the battle has led to girls being seized to become 'wives' for male combatants.

Furaa became a wife after joining an armed group. She was no older than 11. 'It was the first time I knew a man,' she said, adding that she also learnt to fight: 'As I was a sub-officer when they gave me orders to go in front as a soldier, I couldn't ignore them. In one battle they shot me. I found the people in the army group very bad.'

Furaa was eventually sent to a UNICEF transit camp in Goma where she is waiting to return to her community. Reintegrating the children into normal life is difficult. Some people find it hard to accept the return of a girl who has been raped.

Global Report 2008 on the War in the Democratic Republic of the Congo That Began in 1998

Children were recruited and used by all parties to the armed conflict for combat and support roles, and thousands of girls were used as sexual slaves. An estimated 30,000 children were awaiting demobilization from armed forces and other parties to the armed conflict at the end of 2003. Child recruitment by the former Congolese army officially ended in 2003, although some children remained in individual units. National army unification and the national disarmament, demobilization and reintegration (DDR) programs did not begin in earnest until 2005; some 30,000 children had been demobilized by mid-2007. Thousands of others including many girls escaped, were abandoned or left the armed forces without being officially demobilized. From 2005 the UN reported an overall reduction in child-soldier recruitment and use by armed forces and groups—a consequence of a decrease in the number of active fighting zones, the progressive incorporation of armed groups into the national army and the associated demobilization process for adults and children. However, some 7,000 child soldiers remained in armed groups and the Armed Forces of the DRC (Forces armées de la République démocratique du Congo, FARDC). Active recruitment continued in some areas in 2007, particularly in North Kivu.

Coalition to Stop the Use of Child Soldiers,
Child Soldiers: Global Report 2008, *2009.*

'They say rape is a weapon of war,' said Mathenge. When a woman is raped, tradition dictates that her husband must leave her. 'He has no one to cook for him and he has to find a new wife.'

As the girls spoke a white van pulled into the camp. Inside were 14 uniformed boys, all recently demobilised. They had been in one of the myriad rebel groups or the government militia; some had no idea who they had been fighting for.

Cikuru Bishikwabo, the camp's psychologist, said such children fear for their future—'what has happened to their families and village. Being a child soldier destroys the mind. Their language becomes aggressive. They lose the ability to negotiate.'

Later 90 more boys, all former soldiers, turned up in Goma. They were extremely hostile. On arrival, one stole mattresses from a camp and took them to town to sell.

Aid workers say that once a child has been taught to kill it is extremely difficult to remove the violent mentality. In some transit camps girls and boys are kept apart because it is feared the boys will have been taught to rape.

It is the potential for the young to be turned into 'killing machines' that makes them prized by the armies. 'Children are seen as having no fear,' said Dedo Nortey, programme director for Save the Children in neighbouring Rwanda, who works with the Rwandan children sent home from the fighting. 'They follow orders and are easily brainwashed.'

Many of the children admitted they carried out atrocities, killing friends and neighbours when told to do so. Often, as a result, their communities did not want them back.

"Many of the children admitted they carried out atrocities, killing friends and neighbours when told to do so. Often, as a result, their communities did not want them back."

In the camp, Serge was still waiting to return to his village. 'I thought I would go straight home but I spent Christmas and then new year here,' he said. Staff said his father did not want him back.

It is feared that Serge and others like him could become street children. 'Children taken out of the army have ended up on the streets,' said Captain Pascal Kaboy, a logistics officer. 'No one is taking care of them now. That is dangerous because a child who has been used to using a gun can kill people if he does not get what he wants.'

Aid workers, however, insist that they want to overturn a popular idea that it is all right for a child to take up arms and fight.

Marion Turmine, programme director for Save the Children in the country's eastern region, said: 'We need to work with the community to change their mentality—to say that children have the right to play and the right to go to school. To get the children to accept that "I am a child and not a soldier". Reintegration is difficult but I believe it is possible.'

Turmine's team is helping children to reintegrate by setting up projects that provide vocational training. Emmanuele, for instance, is doing a course in masonry. 'I am happy because I am training and will be able to look after my wife,' he said.

And it is not only for former soldiers. They also help other children who have been affected by the war, either through rape or displacement.

Hawa was 13 when three soldiers raped her outside her home. It was another five months before she realised she was pregnant. Now, at 15, with a small child she is finding life difficult: 'I remember I used to go to school,' she said. Hawa has been given two goats and she is being taught to rear them. 'Now I know if I need to I can sell a goat and help my daughter if she becomes sick.'

While the children in the Congo are beginning to receive the aid they desperately need, campaigners in the UK want to ensure the money does not stop too soon.

The Commission for Africa's report warned that half of all countries emerging from conflict relapse into violence within five years. Without decade-long aid for countries which have suffered conflict the former soldiers—now young adults—may return to conflict and in turn recruit a new generation of child warriors.

The names of all the former child soldiers have been changed.

Congo: The Roots of Bloody Conflict. Congo, once the personal fiefdom of King Leopold of Belgium, has been wracked by problems since independence. The popular new Prime Minister, Patrice Lumumba, was arrested and murdered soon after independence, reportedly with US and Belgian complicity. Within four years—in 1965—Joseph Mobutu would launch a coup d'état and rename the country Zaire and himself Mobutu Sese Seko. It would mark the beginning of a looting, remarkable even by Africa's standards, with Mobutu securing a personal fortune of $4 billion.

His time in power was marked by brutality and vast economic incompetence as well as theft. By the mid-1990s his power was waning and by 1997 Tutsi and other anti-Mobutu rebels, aided by Rwanda, captured the capital Kinshasa. Zaire was renamed the Democratic Republic of Congo with Laurent-Désiré Kabila as President.

War continued with six African countries involved in fighting for control of the Congo's valuable resources. While a peace deal was signed in 1999, Kabila, who had done little to improve his country's lot, was assassinated in 2001.

Despite a UN plan to see the pull-out of foreign troops after a conflict that had killed 2.5 million people and a series of peace deals, the violence continued, particularly in eastern Congo. This month a new constitution was agreed by all the warring factions.

Modern Child Soldiers Have Unique Health Concerns

J. Pearn

In the following viewpoint, J. Pearn argues that modern child soldiers have health concerns unique to themselves, different even from child soldiers of the past. Places in which children are used in battle typically do not use international Laws of War. These children—who are often addicted to drugs, impoverished, and suffering from post-traumatic stress disorder—are enmeshed in a cycle of victim-of-violence-perpetrator-of-violence. Pearn argues that because of this cycle of violence, rehabilitating former child soldiers is either impossible or extremely difficult. Pearn is former surgeon general of Australian Defense Force and Royal Children's Hospital in Brisbane, Australia.

As you read, consider the following questions:

1. Historically, what other cultures used children for soldiers?

2. According to the author, what is the most dominant predictor of post-traumatic stress disorder in a person?

3. The author points out that the development of conscience is vital in childhood. What does he say about the child soldier's development of conscience?

Child soldiers comprise a new class of combatants distinct from those of immature years who have, since the times of ancient Greece, served in uniform as an adjunct to former armies and navies. The child soldier of today is enmeshed in a triad of anarchic civil war, light-weight weaponry, and drug or alcohol addiction. One profile of the child soldier of today is a rag-clad, drug-addicted 10- to 18-year-old male carrying an automatic weapon and bonded to a group of other compunctionless combatants led by an older teenager. He lives and kills with impunity and in the absence of identifiable conventions of war or other ethical principles. He acts without the constraints of any regimental tradition. Child soldiers are a unique phenomenon first encountered in the later decades of the twentieth century.

Public health and medicine have traditionally focused on those killed or wounded in battle or on the care of civilians caught in the cross fire of violent political conflict and its aftermath. Since the 1970s, interest has also developed on the identification and care of the psychiatrically scarred among the ranks of both victors and vanquished. Although not traditionally counted among the battle casualties of war, children today are indeed numbered among the victims of each of these categories.

However, today's disciplines of public health and medicine also include study of the plight of child soldiers. The existence of these victims, analogous to those stricken by occupational or industrial disease and morbidity, is due to social forces. And like the plight of other vulnerable populations, the predicament of child soldiers may be understood and addressed by public health approaches: identification of risks, examination of patterns of injury and death, and engagement in effective, concerted prevention, intervention, and advocacy efforts.

There is nothing new about warfare. There has, however, since the establishment of the Red Cross in 1864 and the St. Petersburg Convention of 1869, been an evolution of the international Laws of War in an attempt to alleviate the horrors of war. This has achieved much in the context of international warfare, particularly in conflicts between first-world nations. Less has been achieved in the context of civil wars where the genocide experienced in such places as Bosnia (1991) and Rwanda (1994) has again demonstrated that there is indeed a thin veneer of civilization in contemporary humankind when civil wars erupt. In spite of the ethic of the Geneva Conventions and the influence of the International Red Cross, the Pershing (1921) and Ottawa (1997) Conventions, children and adolescents remain unprotected in many regions of the world where they exist both as perpetrators and victims of combat violence. Children, and particularly orphan children, who are born into and survive in communities that are all but destroyed by civil war, grow and develop both as unprotected victims on the one hand and are subject to recruitment as child soldiers on the other. In both instances, they are not subject to either of the two principal moderating, even humanizing, sanctions of (a) family traditions and (b) civilized, societal mores.

Scholars estimate that there are 300,000 child soldiers in the world today, and they have been involved in over two dozen of the world's armed conflicts since the start of the twenty-first century. These combatants fall into two classes. The first class includes those adolescents who are still voluntarily or semi-voluntarily recruited into the ranks of combatants in armies that subscribe to international codes and principles such as the Geneva Conventions or more generic concepts of the Laws of War. In the past, such children and adolescents have been a proud and important part of the military forces of many nations.

The second class of child soldiers, and the focus of this review, differs from the former group in that there is no formal institutional socialization of such child soldiers. Rather, they may become socialized informally by an ethos that has superficial parallels with urban civilian gangs. The social dynamics of bonded groups of child soldiers, however, differ from those of such urban criminal gangs in at least one very important respect. Criminal gangs remain subject to the sanction of law enforcement and exist within otherwise relatively stable societies. By contrast, child soldiers in their formal or informally bonded groups, do not operate in environments where violent behavior is held in check by the rule of law, law enforcement, or other mechanisms of formal or informal social control. This absence of social controls means that these combatants engage routinely in wanton atrocities and hideously violent acts without remorse or constraint. Consequently, child soldiers often behave to satisfy the dictates of primal gratification rather than to serve as military agents of the state or of organized rebel movements engaged in more traditional forms of warfare or insurgency.

The tragic syndrome of the typical contemporary child soldier involves a boy between the ages of 8 and 16 years, bonded into an armed group of peers. He is almost always an orphan, drug- or alcohol-addicted, amoral, merciless and dangerous, illiterate, and armed with an automatic or semiautomatic weapon and a knife. These combatants rape, steal, and pillage without compunction or remorse. Their targets are never strategic or tactical, but idiosyncratic and personal. The attacks by child soldiers tend to be opportunistic and targets may be either male or female, young or old, civilian or uniformed. The *modus operandi* of killing is often brutal, even mutilatory.

Historical Comparisons

In the preliterate past, adolescent boys after initiation have always taken part in intertribal conflicts as fighting combatants, serving alongside their adult relatives. In recorded history, children have formed part of traditional armies since the fourth century B.C. Some of the best recorded examples relate to the boys of ancient Sparta. Such youths were taught the socially desirable virtues of courage, discipline, self-sufficiency, and resilience, often in the context of extreme training that was demanded of all, irrespective of age, who undertook military service. Unquestionably, many such youths were exploited sexually. Although they were in most cases voluntarily recruited, the term voluntary had little meaning in the absence of child rights and in a context where social pressures and expectations compelled participation.

Armies and navies of the past have always recruited young adolescents. Hospital Apprentice Fitzgibbon, of the Bengal Medical Department, received the Victoria Cross for his action at North Taku Fort, in China, on 21 August, 1860, when he was 15 years of age. Boy Cornwell of the Royal Navy received the award of the Victoria Cross posthumously, for his action at the Battle of Jutland when he was 16 years of age. Both these examples were of child soldiers who were already military veterans in their early teenage years. Many boys under the age of 16 years joined the American Revolutionary (Patriot) Army in 1776.

"The responses of young adolescents to violence and disaster cause profound changes in their attitudes toward life and their future."

In this context of the use of young adolescents as members of traditional armies, many nations have lauded the underage enlistment of teenagers. The untruthful overstating of age, by which young adolescents could go to war, is today usually regarded with paternalistic admiration. The most recent use of this type of formal child soldier was seen in the Iran–Iraq War of 1982–83. In some campaigns in that conflict, young children were used in the vanguard of assaulting troops in the belief that this might deter tactical artillery counter-bombardments.

There has been a progressive evolution among civilized nations and combatant states to forbid the use of young teenagers in combat. The 1998 Statute of the International Criminal Court defined the conscription or enlistment of children under 15 years of age into armed forces for their use in combat as a war crime.

Child Soldiers of the Twenty-First Century

Child soldiers often exist when a society has broken down and anarchy pervades. Under such circumstances, authority is exerted by brute force or its threat. In the twenty-first century, such occurs almost exclusively in civil war contexts or in protracted border disputes between developing nations.

Child soldiering imposes extreme stress. This, in turn, has three profound consequences. The first of these is that the desocialization and dehumanization of a young adolescent's mind become self-perpetuating. The thrill and rush of physical combat, of using powerful weapons, and of domination and sexual conquest intoxicate. Secondly, the lost childhood of such victims means that schooling and rehabilitation are very difficult to institute. This has been very evident in the African experience as the educational rehabilitation of former child soldiers has proven extremely difficult there once the normal window of childhood has closed. Thirdly, many who work with children and adolescents who were child soldiers find high rates of post-traumatic stress disorder (PTSD) among them. Though published work on the long-term mental health and developmental sequelae is lacking, many anticipate that rehabilitation of those once engaged as child soldiers will be difficult if not impossible to achieve.

The responses of young adolescents to violence and disaster cause profound changes in their attitudes toward life and their future. Traumatized adolescents may be especially likely to engage in risky behaviors. Often, in the pre-recruitment phase when a child or young adolescent has already lost parents, siblings, and extended family members, he is particularly vulnerable to enmeshment as a child soldier in societies engaged in long-term political or military conflict. The situation may be compounded by the fact that when parents or other close relatives are lost in massacres, land mine or bomb blasts, or in epidemics, normal rituals of grief and closure do not occur. In the aftermath of conflict, burials and memorialization are a luxury of those civilian societies where the Laws of War still apply.

Young adolescents enmeshed in civil wars are constantly exposed to threats to their own life. This engenders perhaps the highest risk of psychiatric morbidity. Those who are themselves injured by violence or disaster are at highest risk. Exposure to dead bodies and mutilated victims increases the potential for adverse psychiatric sequelae. Of the many different types of stressors, the most powerful predictor of PTSD is direct experience and engagement in physical violence. Children and young adolescents as soldiers and the perpetrators of violence are often simply continuing in the chronological sequence of their entire lifetime experience, themselves having been traumatized as preschool children. Preschool children exposed to violent trauma, even in the civilian sphere, sometimes reenact their trauma in their play and storytelling. Moreover, exposure to violence may alter developmental trajectories and cause other problems with behavior, cognition, emotional status, and social skills. Thus, the milieu in which child soldiers operate represents a high-risk setting for children already damaged by exposure to violence and in which they might have unfortunate and unchecked opportunities to execute violent acts of revenge and aggression ordinarily restricted to play and fantasy.

Violent behavior by male adolescents is highly correlated with prior violent acclimation, even in otherwise stable, civilian, developed nations where violence is eschewed. In a United

Wounded Child Soldiers Often Go Untreated

Health care for wounded child soldiers is often problematic. In most countries where child soldiers are found, health care is at best spotty. Sometimes, both government forces and rebel groups leave the wounded on the battlefield. At times the only medicine available is herbal. The most frequent injuries suffered by child soldiers are loss of hearing, blindness, and loss of limbs. In Guatemala the principal causes of death and injury of minors in the army were said to be the explosion of mines placed by guerillas. This was due to the use of children as advance scouts and as mine detectors. Other causes were grenade, rocket, and bomb explosions.

Physical injury carries additional emotional, psychological, economic, and social disadvantages. Loss of sight or hearing are severe obstacles to educational or social development. Loss of limbs may require repeated amputations for those still growing since the bone of the amputated limb grows more than the surrounding tissue. They will also require new prostheses frequently. In addition to the trauma, treatment costs may be too high or the necessary facilities may be unavailable. In Mozambique demobilized child soldiers complain of health problems related to bullets and shrapnel still lodged in their bodies. Many families do not have the resources to pay for operations to remove these objects. In societies with high levels of unemployment, the additional disadvantages from wounds may be too hard to overcome.

David Isenberg, "The Invisible Soldiers: Child Combatants,"
Defense Monitor, *July 1997.*

States study from Yale, it was shown that there exists a very high correlation between prior violent victimization and later perpetration of physical assault. Adolescent males in particular are likely to reenact their own experiences of violent victimization by perpetrating similar forms of violence on others.

There are no quantitative research reports about violence exposure among child soldiers. Methodological challenges rule the day. Almost all child soldiers are illiterate, the contexts they exist within are extremely volatile and dangerous, and the social destruction of civil wars where they thrive make defining and obtaining representative samples difficult if not impossible.

However, journalistic accounts, reports of nongovernmental organizations and first-person narratives like Ismael Beah's *A Long Way Gone: Memoirs of a Boy Soldier* (2007) grant important insights into this emerging problem.

"Child soldiers have almost never been to school and almost all are illiterate."

Aftermath and Rehabilitation

Child soldiers have almost never been to school and almost all are illiterate. The harm and disabilities from this denial of a basic human right have lifelong consequences. For example, in the context of the 2001 war in Afghanistan, the *Wall Street Journal* reported that "A key issue is what to do with thousands of young men who have, over two decades of conflict in Afghanistan, learned little more than how to pull a trigger" (p. A14).

Some adolescents exposed to violent trauma respond by developing a perspective and outlook that life will be short and that a fragile, shortened future marked by suffering and vulnerability is their inevitable lot. Under such circumstances, they often spiral downward into a maelstrom of hedonism and hopelessness.

Many children enmeshed in war develop fear-conditioned responses to early experiences of violence. As adolescents they may regress or engage in aggressive behavior throughout their lives. While many normal adults without traumatic histories of exposure to violence have flashbacks triggered by the smell of certain foods or plants, these hippocampus-mediated responses are often pleasurable. However, for survivors exposed to violence or war during childhood, their olfactory triggers are the stench of burning flesh, bloody wounds, or explosives. Some postulate that flashbacks induced in these ways result from neural short circuits of the rhinencephalon—the atavistic remnants of the highly developed sense of smell memories of lower animals. But whatever the mechanisms, experiences of war and violence can make their mark extremely early in life, indelibly, and even prior to consciousness. In this way, many communities embroiled in long-term violent political conflict may produce children who have been affected by war long before they become weapon-carrying combatants themselves. For example, research into the aftermath of the Bosnia-Croatia conflict of 1995 showed that the average birth weight and nutritional indices of breastfed infants were reduced during periods of continued immediate combat threat.

Of sinister import is that children chronically exposed to the injury and death of war may carry a unique and dangerous datum reference point into their adult lives: that violence is the fundamental relationship that characterizes human interaction. Perhaps this is why studies of child survivors of the Spanish Civil War of 1936, the Nazi Holocaust, and the London Blitz have revealed that they grow up to be adults more inured than their unexposed peers to the horrors of violence.

One of the most important tasks of normal childhood is the development of conscience, that is, the acquisition of a sense of higher-order morality and ethics. Among child soldiers, the development of this sense of right and wrong is either never attained or is lost in the absence of normal influences of family and society.

Advocacy. Children are sometimes injured or killed in war by its direct effects: blast, bomb, missile, burns, or gas. Larger numbers suffer or die from exposure to the elements or from disease and starvation. Just like other calamities—earthquakes, famine, cyclones, and epidemic pestilence—war is another type of social catastrophe that destroys families, communities, and societies. Just as in these other disasters, the problem of child soldiers can be ameliorated by approaches common to public health and preventive medicine. Advocacy can make a difference here as well.

The humanitarian work of nongovernmental organizations (NGOs) does much to rehabilitate child soldiers. Some term these efforts demobilization, disarmament, and reintegration programs (DDR). However, one of the great challenges of these efforts is that surviving child soldiers often return to brittle, depleted, post-conflict societies. The survivors may be hard to identify and the road to recovery is long and difficult. These realities elevate the importance of prevention, a task which requires vigorous national and international advocacy.

International advocacy has done much to protect the plight of civilians (the third Geneva Convention), to achieve considerable reduction in the use of chemical warfare (the Pershing Convention of 1921), and to offer partial protection to future generations by the Ottawa Convention (1997) by which an increasing number of nations have become signatories to the banning of the manufacture and international sale of antipersonnel land mines. The 1972 Biological and Toxin Weapons Convention banned the development of biological weapons for offensive purposes. Although it was violated by several nations, its spirit is implicitly accepted by all governments today. Professor John Steinburner, Professor of Public Policy at the University of Maryland, has described it as "arguably among the most significant universal rules of human civilization," (Steinburner J, 2006: 20).

To this pantheon of conventions has been added one of great significance. This is the convention to ban child soldiers. The International Criminal Court by its 1998 Statute (also known as the Rome Statute) bans the conscription and enlistment of children aged under 15 years into armed forces for use in combat and other military activities such as scouting, spying, sabotage, and use as couriers and decoys or at checkpoints. In addition, the ILO Worst Forms of Child Labor Convention 182, enacted in 2000, commits states which ratify it to take measures to prohibit and eliminate the "worst forms of child labor," which include use in armed conflict. Moreover, the recruitment and use of any person under age 15 years in armed conflict is prohibited by Article 38 of the Convention on the Rights of the Child (the Optional Protocol of the CRC enacted in 2002 raised the minimum age of use in armed conflict to 18 years). Like all such international conventions and rules, there will continue to be violations. Nevertheless, the legal infrastructure to prevent child soldiers now in place is a global standard against which interventions can be evaluated and toward which advocacy can be directed. Ongoing national and international advocacy to prevent, ban, and rehabilitate child soldiers has become a critical global humanitarian and public health goal and is the way forward.

See also: Child Rights; Child Witness to Violence; Ethnic Conflict and Public Health; Torture and Public Health.

Citations

Newman S (2001) Will Afghans give up their weapons? Many carry Kalashnikofs after years of civil war. *Wall Street Journal International* 228: A14.

Steinburner J (2006) In the name of defence. *New Scientist* 192: 20.

Further Reading

Bodman F (1941) War conditions and the mental health of the child. *British Medical Journal* 12: 468–488.

Chimienti G, Nasr JA, and Khalifeh I (1989) Children's reactions to war-related stress. *Social Psychiatry and Psychiatric Epidemiology* 24: 282–287.

McWhirter L (1983) Northern Ireland: Growing up with the 'troubles'. In: Goldstein AP and Segall MH (eds.) *Aggression in Global Perspective*, pp. 367–400. New York: Permagon Press.

Pearn JH (1996) War zone paediatrics in Rwanda. *Journal of Paediatrics and Child Health* 32: 290–295.

Pearn JH (2003) Children and War. *Journal of Paediatrics and Child Health* 39: 166–172.

Schaller JG and Nightingale EO (1992) Editorial. Children and childhoods. Hidden casualties of war and civil unrest. *Journal of the American Medical Association* 268: 642–644.

Former Child Soldiers Benefit from Indigenous Cultural Practices of Healing

Zulfiya Tursunova

In the following viewpoint, Zulfiya Tursunova argues that when attempting to reintegrate child soldiers into communities, Western approaches alone do not work. Instead, indigenous rituals must be recognized as valid ways to promote healing. While Western psychologists often promote individual counseling as a way to heal from traumatic experiences, many indigenous communities view trauma as a shared community experience. Therefore, communities must be involved in healing former child soldiers. Tursunova is a lecturer and trainer on peace education, gender migration, and development issues.

As you read, consider the following questions:

1. According to some indigenous cultures, why must cleansing rituals be used to wash away evil spirits of people killed in war?

2. How is the perception of adulthood different in rural sub-Saharan Africa than in Western countries?

3. What example is given of a way in which female soldiers experience double discrimination once they are released?

Zulfiya Tursunova, "The Role of Rituals in Healing Trauma and Reconciliation in Post-Accord Peacebuilding," *Journal of Human Security*, vol. 4, no. 3, December 2008, pp. 54–72. Copyright © 2008 RMIT Publishing. Reproduced by permission.

Civilians have always been targeted in war, in particular children. Worldwide, more than 300,000 children are involved in armed conflicts with government armies, paramilitaries, and other types of militarised groups. Children become the victims of war and are exploited as child soldiers, cooks, couriers, spies and also serve as providers of sexual services. In times of war, children perform combatant tasks or, we can say, war rituals: murdering, abducting people, robbing houses and people, and burning villages. . . . Some people consider ex-soldiers as hardened killers who have been abused and forced to do violence, and have become 'damaged goods,' and thus have little chance of reintegrating into communities or recovering. . . . According to traditional belief, people who murder or see people being murdered become contaminated spiritually because contamination originates from contact with death and bloodshed. Those people become polluted by the spirits of dead persons and are likely to contaminate the social body.

In times of crisis, rituals perform a significant role in healing children affected by war. Contrary to traditional Western approaches of social workers or psychologists who advocate counselling or verbalising traumatic experiences, many indigenous communities consider trauma as a shared collective experience. Cleansing rituals help to wash away the evil spirits of the people killed, which are deemed to hang around the soldier who murdered them and can bring illnesses, bad luck, and infertility. Indigenous people regard spiritual impurity as a threat, and consequently are willing to reestablish harmony between ex-soldiers and community members and the ancestors. In rural Africa, community healers conduct rituals to expunge bad spirits and heal. In spite of the criticism of healing rituals that do not ensure long-term psychological healing to child soldiers, it is widely acknowledged that healing and reintegration strategies should be based on local practices to be sustainable and effective. The social integration should be accompanied with social development to reduce poverty. . . .

Defining "Adult" According to Culture

Child recruitment is considered a crime under international law, and a crime against humanity. The international community raised its concern to develop legal frameworks on the use of child soldiers in conflict zones. Many efforts have been put into raising the minimum legal age of recruitment. The age limit of child soldiering is endorsed by the Convention on the Rights of Children (CRC), the worldwide human rights instrument. It is based on the Western notion of the term 'child' and the Western developmental science which considers an individual under the age of 18 to be a child. However, understanding the term 'child' varies from culture to culture. The Coalition to Stop the Use of Child Soldiers indicates that international standards determining the age of a child under 18 differ from local concepts. The debates arise around 'rites of passage' such as marriage and the voting age which in some countries can be below the age of 18. It is also argued that in impoverished or war-torn countries, children have to take the responsibilities of adults in order for their families to survive. I use the term child soldier bearing in mind that Western cultural understanding of the definition of the child soldier is highly contested in other cultures.

In rural areas in sub-Saharan Africa an individual is considered to be an adult when she/he carries out the traditional initiation ceremonies or rites of passage into womanhood and manhood. In Sudan, a boy who participates in the initiation ceremony is regarded as adult, and may be considered eligible for recruitment by armed forces, or by volunteering himself. Yet, being a child may not always necessarily have a connection to the age limit but has a direct connection to one's social roles, expectations, and responsibilities. In Angola, among the Tchokwe, children are identified by the roles performed, and are named according to their activities. For example, tchi-tutasare boys and girls from the age of five to seven; they fetch tobacco and water to elders and also deliver messages to community members. Kambubmbu are children, in particular girls, from seven to thirteen years of age, who fulfill household work, help parents with agricultural work, hunting and fishing. Mukwenge wa lunga (boys) and the mwana pwo (girls) at about the age of thirteen perform the rites of initiation. In Mozambique, girls at around the age of thirteen become wives and soon have children. In these sociocultural contexts, the accent is put on the roles rather than on the age.

Therefore, armed groups may not be willing to accept the legal concept of child soldier and prefer to favour such terms as 'separated children' or 'children under the care of the group.' In this situation, the use of children may reveal cultural values of community that must be dealt with during interventions and facilitate the required long-term protection of children from recruitment and use. The release of children and in general the main priority of the protection of children demands flexibility and the ability to apply law as a tool in cases when it contributes to the protection of child soldiers....

"Healing extends beyond the trauma of the person and decreases the social divisions existing within and between communities."

Reintegration of Male Child Soldiers

War-affected rural communities in Mozambique and Angola apply a variety of traditional rituals to deal with traumas of war and set up a way for reconciliation. Rituals address the challenge of healing the psychosocial traumas related to war and upheaval. Trauma contains different sufferings which have impacted soldiers, children, females and all other community members caught up in the war in different circumstances. Healing extends beyond the trauma of a person and decreases the social divisions existing within and between communities. During the ritual, the child soldier is cleansed from the pollution of war and death, and sin and guilt, and is guarded from retaliation by the spirits of the killed soldier. The peculiarities of ceremonies may vary depending on the ethno-linguistic group, but their topics are universal to all groups in Mozambique and Angola.

A family planned a ritual for their son Pitango from Cambandua in Angola, who had been in the armed forces for three years and returned home at the age of eighteen. The ceremony began one day before he came back, and he was permitted to socialise with community members and relatives. Pitango's body was washed with cassava meal. A chicken was killed and its blood was put on his forehead. His mother took some palm oil and rubbed it on her son's hands and feet. During the ceremony, the family called the spirits of ancestors to defend the young man. The elders of the relatives performed a prayer as they were closest to the ancestors because of age.

In Angola, a greeting ritual is carried out by the community to cleanse the boy soldiers of spiritual pollutions. Women get ready for the ceremony; some part of the flour used by women to paint their foreheads is tossed on a child and an older woman tosses a gourd filled with ashes at the child's feet. At the same time, clean water is thrown over a boy as a way of purification. The women of the community dance near the child and gesture with their hands to send away the bad spirits. Women touch the boy from head to foot to purify him. When the ceremony is over, the child is welcomed to his village to celebrate his arrival. A celebration is held at his house with customary drinks. The child's parents introduce their child to the chiefs formally. The child sits next to the chiefs, drinks and talks to them. This action transforms the change of the status of the child in the village. This act transforms a child's identity from a child soldier to a community member.

In Huambo, Angola, when a child soldier returns home, before entering the house he is supposed to step first on the egg of a chicken (elembui) that is put in the doorway. The symbolic meaning of the broken egg is that the child moves away from the past and the eviction of the spirits that might haunt the soldier. Another ceremony involves killing a chicken and letting the child jump over the chicken while it is shaking. After that, the boy is bathed with water before going into the house. Another ritual is that a pot of water is broken between the legs of a soldier. Usually, the mother carries out this act and says 'Onhassa' to send the spirits away and let the child become as pure as the water spilled on his feet. In the province of Moxico, the returning soldier is met with a cheerful celebration. The relatives and community members throw fuba maize meal on his head and face as a symbol of thankfulness to the spirits that safeguarded him. In the case of ex-soldiers who demonstrate signs of disturbances, special healing rituals are performed. A similar ritual is carried out in Bie province. An animal is killed and sacrificed as a meal to the spirits that protected a child. The youth throw fuba maize meal on to the child's head and rub palm oil into the child's hands. There are two parts in welcoming the child soldier: an act of meeting which consists of the purification of the ex-child soldier and a ritual of removal from the past; and a ritual of healing which entails cleansing and protection. These parts can be separate or joined together in one ceremony. . . .

Symbolism Is Used to Reveal Life and Spirit

In another ritual in rural Angola, the healer uses burning leaves of a sacred herb to identify the place that bad spirits cannot inhabit. The healer makes the former boy soldier breathe the fumes; he rubs the boy's chest and back with roots that are thought to eradicate bad spirits and prevent their re-entry. The healer, to appease the bad spirits, provides food

---

Locking the Past Away

The boy, dressed with the dirty clothes he brought from the . . . camp, entered the hut and undressed himself. Then fire was set to the hut, and an adult relative helped out the boy. The hut, the clothes and everything else that the boy brought from the camp had to be burned. A chicken was sacrificed for the spirits of the dead and the blood spread around the ritual place. After that the boy had to inhale the smoke of some herbal remedies, and bath himself with water treated with medicine.

This healing ritual brings together a series of symbolic meanings aimed at cutting the child's link with the past (the war). While modern psychotherapeutic practices emphasize verbal exteriorization of the affliction, here through symbolic meanings the past is locked away. This is seen in the burning of the hut and the clothes and the cleansing of the body. To talk and recall the past is not necessarily seen as a prelude to healing or diminishing pain. Indeed, it is often believed to open the space for the malevolent forces to intervene.

Edward C. Green and Alcinda Honwana,
"Indigenous Healing of War Affected Children in Africa,"
Africa Action, July 1999.

---

and traditional liquor which is put around the safe place. He also sacrifices a chicken. At the end of the ritual, the boy jumps out of the room which implies that all contaminations are left behind, the boy is purified and accepted from this moment onward. This ritual is carried out to deal with severe impurities such as killing people, whose angry spirits can chase the boy.

In rural Mozambique, the spirits of the people killed by the fighters or civilians are called Mpfhukwa. These spirits haunt people and can punish them if they do not receive the necessary burial rites to settle in the next world; they can be nasty to people who crossed their path. Mpfhukwa spirits have a capacity to distress, cause illness and even kill people who did not treat them well when they were alive. Moreover, the power of these spirits can pass on to the family members.

Rituals to reconcile with Mpfhukwa are mostly carried out by Tinyanga, local spirits mediums who know how to catch, take away or appease them. The ceremony is performed at the place where people perished or at the battlefield. In April 1993, the Tinyanga from Munguine village in the province of Manica carried out a ritual along the road connecting Munguine to Manhiça village. The spirit of the Renamo commander who was killed at this place prevented people from using the road when it became dark. People told that when they took this road, they felt that something was punching them; they heard voices asking them to go back, otherwise they would become blind and could not see their way home. The spirit asked for money and capulanas (traditional cloths) and a need to be taken to his home to Ndauland. The villagers collected money and bought the cloths to offer to the spirits. In one week, the spirit was caught again and tied with fabric and buried with the money far from the villages. The Tinyanga also put medicine in the pieces of fabric to bar the spirits' return. The local people said that after the ritual had been performed they had not experienced any problems along that road. These rituals with symbols involved garments and sacred medicine to change the order in which individuals think. Symbols are not only the means by which we think, rather symbols reorder the way in which we think.

Reintegration of Female Child Soldiers

The efforts to deal with Disarmament, Demobilization, and Reintegration (DDR) should take into account the root causes of the conflict: the nature of warfare, collapse of rule and order, poverty, unemployment, inequality, poor education and other forms of exclusion. Rehabilitation programs should be grounded on gender-sensitive approaches and take into account the needs of female soldiers and the sociocultural milieu [setting]. Girls in the Democratic Republic of the Congo (DRC) performed different roles: combat duties, cooking responsibilities, and providing medical help. Thousands were raped and abused and have children as the result of rape. Military rulers and fighters quite often take for granted the possession of girls naming them 'wives.' Thus, they do not take any responsibility to release the girls for demobilisation. The National DDR Commission stated that in May 2006, of the total of 18,500 demobilised children, only 2,900 (15 percent) constituted girls. In El Salvador 11 percent of demobilised soldiers were women, while in Sierra Leone 8 percent of the soldiers were female.

Female soldiers experience double discrimination upon their release in the DDR. For example, in Sierra Leone, the child soldiers who had a demobilisation number were waived school fees. In addition, the schools accepting child soldiers received a package of educational materials designed for all students to promote inclusion of child soldiers. Female soldiers who did not demobilise officially did not receive any kind of benefits.

> *"Girls are subjected to multiple methods of discrimination. . . . Many become beggars or rejoin armed groups."*

In Sierra Leone the soldiers raped many women. The situation of the child soldiers was difficult because of the stigma attached. In Sierra Leone, the bush is considered a sacred place of the ancestors. The rural people regarded rape as the violation of sacredness that made girls spiritually contaminated which brings misfortune to their families and to agricultural crops. The villagers were afraid of girls, ridiculed them, and called them names and sometimes assaulted them.

Many girls prefer not to go through the rehabilitation programs fearing stigmatisation. As a result, they do not access reintegration programs and become vulnerable to new recruitment. Some girls who came home were rejected by family members and the community for their sexual activity. Girls are subjected to multiple methods of discrimination, during the conflict, at the moment of demobilisation, and upon coming back into their communities. Consequently, they link themselves to prostitution networks, many become beggars or rejoin armed groups.

In Sierra Leone, performing specific rituals is a crucial part of community reconciliation with returning youth soldiers. In most communities, a local healer performs a purification ritual that allows taking away the young girls' contamination and enabling them to reintegrate into the community. In Sierra Leone, the purification rituals differed from region to region yet had common features, such as the ritual of washing girls by scrubbing with special leaves and black soap in the river. The foam produced from scrubbing was assumed to remove impurities of the body, letting the river wash them away. One healer in a village applied a fumigation method; the girl drank a mixture of boiled herbs and then inhaled the vapor under the blanket. Wearing the dress of a particular colour was also a main symbolic element in the ritual. The girls wore a white cloth on their heads and a red cloth on their hips while sitting on a mat covered with cowry shells. The healer and the girls ate food together prepared specifically for this occasion. After that, they danced and drummed all night. In the morning, the girls were wrapped in the white cloth which symbolised purity. The healer presented the girls purified 'new' to the villagers. The healer and parents have some conversation, and the girls are welcomed by local people amidst drumming, singing, and dancing.

Colombia's Child Soldiers Join Rebels to Escape Poverty

Helen Murphy

In the following viewpoint, Helen Murphy explains how poverty affects Colombian youths' decisions to join the rebels and fight. The Revolutionary Armed Forces of Colombia (FARC) promises food and protection. But once children and teens join, they are traumatized by the killing and not allowed to express fear. Worse, once they join, the young soldiers are in for life with no way out but death. Murphy is a journalist for Bloomberg.com.

As you read, consider the following questions:

1. According to the author, how might the global financial crisis impact Colombia's armed conflict?
2. Why did Juan join the Revolutionary Armed Forces of Colombia (FARC)?
3. What type of group was the FARC when it was originally founded?

Struggling through the tangled jungle with his AK-47 rifle loaded and ready, 16-year-old Juan thought only of his mother, a clean bed and freedom as 15 armed guerrillas closed in to kill him.

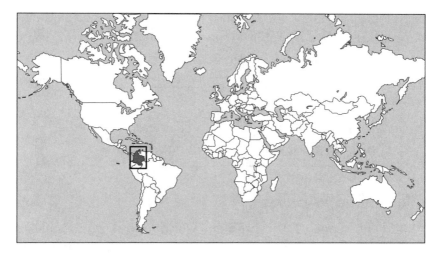

Just an hour earlier, he had been their comrade, fighting alongside them as a member of the Revolutionary Armed Forces of Colombia, or FARC. As a deserter, he faced execution.

"I couldn't take the fear and hunger any more," recalls Juan, a physically and emotionally scarred former child soldier who turned himself in to Colombia's military in 2008 after escaping from two years with the drug-funded rebels. "The army bombed us every night and I was afraid."

As the world seeks to prevent the use of minors in armed conflict, thousands—some as young as 11—bear arms in Colombia's illegal forces, according to New York-based Human Rights Watch. The global financial crisis may increase the pool of willing recruits: With more rural Colombians facing poverty, it may be easier for the rebels to replace members killed or captured in President Álvaro Uribe's attacks against them.

Young prospects "come from poor and brutal backgrounds, where even armed combat seems a better option, and the FARC is happy to take them in," says Philippe Houdard, whose

Developing Minds Foundation in Miami Beach, Florida, helps fund a home in Colombia for former child combatants, some of whom were forced into service.

"'Some told me they lost control of their bowels in combat. But they are not allowed to be afraid; they would be ridiculed by those they depend on for survival.'"

"Appalling" Abuses

While the scope of the problem worldwide is impossible to gauge, Lucia Withers, acting director of the London-based Coalition to Stop the Use of Child Soldiers, says youngsters are always involved in wars in some way. United Nations Secretary-General Ban Ki-moon on Feb. 12 [2009] said the use of child soldiers is "one of the most appalling human rights abuses in the world today."

Once the killing starts, "they are thrown into extreme stress," says Maggie Mauer, a Coral Gables, Florida, psychologist who has studied Colombia's former young fighters. "Some told me they lost control of their bowels in combat. But they are not allowed to be afraid; they would be ridiculed by those they depend on for survival."

Juan, who bears a deep gouge down his left cheek, joined the FARC, Colombia's largest illegal armed group, when he was 14. Like most young recruits, he came voluntarily with the promise of adventure and a better life away from destitution. He also wanted revenge on the army for killing his older brother, another child soldier. . . .

Poverty and parental abuse are the overriding reasons for joining the FARC, says Beatriz Linares, who heads the government's effort to prevent child recruitment. The group often tricks families into believing they will be paid if their sons and daughters enlist, she says.

There Are No Childhood Dreams Here

I once sat outside a village school in eastern Colombia with 15 youngsters who said they had left the FARC [Revolutionary Armed Forces of Colombia]—at the order of guerrilla commanders—to return to school.

I asked them what they wanted to be when they grow up. Dead silence. Firemen, doctors, vets, astronauts? I inquired. But in that corner of Colombia children don't have childhood dreams. They laughed and made me feel stupid.

Karl Penhaul,
"Haunted by Seeing Dead and Killing People,"
CNN International, *June 9, 2006.*

Some 45 percent of Colombia's 44 million inhabitants lived below the poverty line of 232,000 pesos ($97) a month in 2006, according to the most recent data from the national planning department.

The FARC was founded in 1964 as a peasant-based, Marxist group. According to defense ministry estimates, its ranks have been halved to about 8,000 since Uribe took office in 2002. That's partly because of his commitment to defeat drug-funded rebel groups and partly because of desertion.

"It seems to be difficult for the FARC to recruit adults at the moment, but children, who know less about what they're getting into, are much easier targets," says Maria McFarland, senior researcher for Latin America at Human Rights Watch.

Death Is the Only Way Out

Miguel, 18 years old, left his parents' coca farm at 13 to join about 300 FARC fighters in Guaviare, central Colombia. He says he "was bored" working with his father picking coca leaves, the raw material for making cocaine, and processing them into base before selling it to the FARC.

"The militia passed our farm all the time, and I dreamt of joining them and getting a gun," he says.

The local FARC leader, accustomed to the attraction of holding a weapon, gave Miguel eight days to consider his decision—warning that, once in the ranks, there was no way out except death, Miguel says.

He decided to march 10 days into the mountains to join the guerrillas that would be his family for the next three years. They gave him camouflaged fatigues, a pistol and a space on the jungle floor to sleep. Months later he would get his prized AK-47 and lessons on how to kill with it.

Life the first few months was good, he says. He was split off from the main FARC front into a smaller command of 60, at least half of whom were under 16. He got an alias—a way of remaining anonymous and protecting the group—a 75-pound equipment backpack and a plastic sheet to protect him from the rain. He was trained in making and burying land mines, running drugs and standing guard.

"At the beginning, the only thing that bothered us was the mosquitoes," Miguel says. "Then I got homesick, as most do, and the commander watched us like a hawk. If he suspected we were going to escape, he would have us shot. We lived in terror."

One friend was just 15 when the FARC riddled him with 50 bullets for trying to flee.

"That hit me hard," says Miguel, who was shot in the chest and lost the use of his left arm in combat. "I wanted him to escape so he could tell my mother I was okay." He surrendered to the army when he was 16 after being surrounded in a gun battle.

No More Choices

Child soldiers are trained to take part in war trials and discipline their peers, says Human Rights Watch's McFarland.

"They made us vote to kill our comrades, and if we didn't raise our hands, we were in danger, too," says Mario, 18, who joined the FARC when he was 14.

"Child soldiers are trained to take part in war trials and discipline their peers."

Juan, who is learning to machine stitch garments at a safe house in Colombia, says he was forced to watch as a 17-year-old dug his own grave and was shot by a 19-year-old female rebel for a series of infractions that included falling asleep on guard duty.

While the FARC calls itself the people's army, fighting for the rights of the rural poor, Juan, now 17, says ideological training was scarce.

"We were narcos," he says, biting his gnarled fingernails and wringing his hands. "We marched, we cooked, we fought, but we never did anything for the Colombian people."

With young men and women in the ranks, romance and pregnancy is discouraged. While overt sexual abuse isn't tolerated, underage female guerrillas are often pressured into sexual relations and forced to use contraceptives. Many babies are aborted.

"The girls are just too young to consent," McFarland says.

Since 1999, Colombia's government-run social services have helped almost 4,000 young fighters who left illegal rebel groups. In addition to providing job training, the services also assist in their return to society, which can be difficult, according to Developing Minds' Houdard.

"They are psychologically battle-scarred and know only violence," he says. "Encouraging them to stay away from crime and violence once they leave is the biggest challenge of all."

Carlos, 17, hopes for "a better life" after spending four years with the FARC. "But if I have to go back again, or into another criminal band, I will. I really haven't got too much choice."

In Iraq, Child Soldiers Want to Be Martyrs

Toby Harnden

The following viewpoint examines why young Iraqi boys are drawn to war. Encouraged by their parents and other members of their communities, Toby Harnden asserts that teenage boys choose to fight because of promised spiritual rewards waiting for them in heaven. Iraqis who defend the use of child soldiers claim it is a positive thing to have old and young fighting side by side. But as the numbers of resistance soldiers dwindle, the numbers of child soldiers rise, and the age of child soldiers decreases. Harnden is the Telegraph's *U.S. editor, based in Washington, D.C.*

As you read, consider the following questions:

1. According to Toby Harnden, who is the head of Shia Islam in Iraq?
2. What were the signs that indicated everything was not going Sheikh Ahmad al-Sheibani's way?
3. Why did the Iraqi militiamen grow distrustful of the media?

Struggling to lift a Kalashnikov [a Soviet-made assault rifle], a 12-year-old with the Mahdi army militia said he could do anything in battle except fly a helicopter. . . .

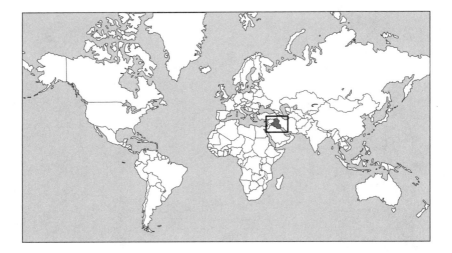

"Last night I fired a rocket-propelled grenade against a tank," he said. "The Americans are weak. They fight for money and status and squeal like pigs when they die.

"But we will kill the unbelievers because faith is the most powerful weapon."

The boy called himself Moqtada, styled after the rebel cleric [religious leader] whose ranks he joined a month ago having travelled to Najaf from the Shia slum of Sadr City in Baghdad. He said that he hopes for a glorious death.

"'We will kill the unbelievers because faith is the most powerful weapon.'"

There are many more child soldiers in the narrow alleyways of the old city that surrounds the 11th-century Imam Ali shrine, its golden dome marking the mausoleum of Shia Islam's martyred founder and son-in-law of the prophet Mohammed.

US armoured vehicles were seen yesterday [August 22, 2004] within 400 yards of the shrine.

The American military appears to be moving closer and closer so that a swift all-out assault can be launched.

The Effects of War on the 13 Million Children of Iraq

Orphaned	4–5 million
Living on the street	500,000
Suffering from malnutrition	400,000
Addicted to drugs (in Baghdad alone)	11,000
Working as child laborers	over 1 million
Held in detention centers (for acting as child soldiers)	1,500
Not attending school (primary school age)	6.5 million
No access to clean drinking water	7.8 million

TAKEN FROM: "Iraq: An Intolerable Situation for Iraqi Children," Children and Armed Conflict, April 25, 2008. http://www.un.org; "Iraq: An 'Intolerable Place for Children,'" CRIN: Child Rights Information Network, April 25, 2008. http://www.ombudsnet.org.

Sheikh Ahmad al-Sheibani, spokesman for Moqtada al-Sadr, the cleric who commands the Mahdi army, yesterday held out little hope of an imminent peaceful solution to the 18-day battle.

The outcome of the siege is crucial to the success of the fledgling government in Iraq and it had been hoped that an offer by the rebels to hand over the keys of the mosque to Shia Islam leaders might break the stalemate.

However, the keys remain with the rebels. Apparently a committee to ponder the matter would have to be set up before any keys could be surrendered to Grand Ayatollah Ali al-Sistani, the living head of Shia Islam in Iraq and a figure much more revered than Sadr.

Sheikh Sheibani defended the use of child soldiers in battle.

"This shows that the Mahdi are a popular resistance movement against the occupiers," he said. "The old men and the young men are on the same field of battle. The oldest is about 60 and the youngest perhaps 15."

A Time for Death

The open courtyard surrounding the shrine was strangely se-
rene yesterday, despite gunfire nearby and the thump of the
odd tank shell. Beneath the golden pillars, young men challenged reporters to arm-wrestling contests and borrowed sat-
ellite phones so that they could call relatives.

Waiters from the nearby—and empty—pilgrim hotels
brought platters of chicken and rice. A temporary hospital was
stacked with boxes of medical supplies, labelled "Italian Red
Cross" and, in Austrian, "Society Iraq Relief". It had been
treating militiamen wounded in the firefights with Iraqi and
American forces. Yesterday, however, it had only one patient,
who was being treated for shrapnel wounds.

But despite Sheikh Sheibani's assertion that "no political
process in Iraq can be successful without the involvement of
Moqtada al-Sadr", there were signs that not everything was
going the militant cleric's way. The number of "human shields"
who had travelled from all over Iraq to protect the shrine had
dwindled from about 2,000 a week earlier to around 200.

---

*"'I would prefer to live and taste victory but if not my
death will be rewarded with spiritual gifts in heaven.'"*

The use of 12-year-olds, armed and apparently ready for
the ranks, also suggests a shortage of seasoned fighters.

There was also a sense of growing tension among the militiamen, who had previously been almost jocular with the
media but yesterday accused some reporters of being intelligence agents.

"You are spies," one veteran said. "Yesterday you betrayed
our whereabouts to the Americans."

His eight-strong unit included another young boy, armed
with a Russian PKC machine gun. It was preparing an SPG 9
rocket launcher to use against American tanks, which could be
heard just outside the compound on the main road.

A wire ran from the doorway where they had gathered, out of the street and around a concrete pillar 30 yards away that was apparently rigged with explosives.

There were also fewer fighters around than in previous days, a sign perhaps that the American tactic of attrition was working or that the pre-dawn bombardment of the ravaged area just outside the Old City had exhausted the militiamen, if not the boys.

"My parents encouraged me to come here," said Malik, a boy of about 14 from the southern Shia city of Diwaniyah.

"I would prefer to live and taste victory but if not my death will be rewarded with spiritual gifts in heaven."

Little Moqtada agreed. "I am young and there is a time for playing football and enjoying myself," he said. "But there is also a time for death."

Periodical Bibliography

BBC News   "Alarm over Somalia's Child Soldiers," July 29, 2009. http://news.bbc.co.uk.

Nina Bernstein   "Taking the War Out of a Child Soldier," *New York Times Upfront*, September 3, 2007.

Sheryl   "The Devil's Yoke: A Young Woman Describes
Henderson Blunt   Her Former Life as a Slave of Rebel Soldiers," *Christianity Today*, March 2007.

John Boonstra   "How Much Shame Can Child Murderers Really Have?" UN Dispatch, August 5, 2009. www.undispatch.com.

Roméo Dallaire, as   "Retired Lieutenant General Roméo Dallaire
told to Kate Fillion   Talks About the 'Value' of Girl Soldiers, and Life Post-Rwanda," *Maclean's*, March 12, 2007.

Economist   "Child Soldiers in Sri Lanka: Retraining Tiger Cubs," July 16, 2009.

Annie Kelly   "Agony Without End for Liberia's Child Soldiers," *Guardian*, July 12, 2009. www.guardian.co.uk.

Thomas Roberts   "Children Forced to Kill," *National Catholic Reporter*, May 13, 2005.

Sonali Salgado   "Rights-Sudan: 'We Really Need Some Political Will,'" IPS, August 6, 2009. www.ipsnews.net.

SOS Children's   "Warlords Recruit Somali Child Soldiers,"
Villages Canada   July 29, 2009. www.soschildrensvillages.ca.

Sudan Tribune   "36 Child Soldiers Demobilized in North Darfur," July 28 2009. www.sudantribune.com.

VOA News   "Taliban Child Soldiers," August 7, 2009. www.voanews.com.

VOA News   "Trafficking—Child Soldiers," July 12, 2009. www.voanews.com.

GLOBALVIEWPOINTS

CHAPTER 3

Efforts to End the Use of Children as Soldiers

International Efforts to Combat Child Soldiers Are Not Enough

UN General Assembly, Social, Humanitarian and Cultural Affairs Committee

In the following viewpoint, former child soldier Ishmael Beah expresses disappointment to United Nations representatives in their handling of the dilemma of children living in conflict. According to Beah, the UN has done very little to follow through on promises made a decade previous to place these children at the top of their agenda. International representatives respond to Beah's criticism with acknowledgment of their neglect and promises to do more.

As you read, consider the following questions:

1. Who is Ann M. Veneman?
2. What document is the most quickly and widely ratified human rights instrument?
3. In what ways is the situation of children in sub-Saharan Africa a source of major concern?

A former child soldier in Sierra Leone turned best-selling author took the international community to task today [October 17, 2007] for failing to do more for children living amid conflict, as the Third Committee (Social, Humanitarian and Cultural) began its discussion on the rights of children this afternoon.

Ishmael Beah, who as a young teenager had been forced to fight in the civil war in his country in the 1990s, recalled how hopeful the mood had been when he came to the United Nations a decade ago to draw attention to the plight of young people caught up in war. That appearance coincided with the publication of a landmark United Nations report by Graça Machel that put children in conflict at the forefront of the Organization's agenda.

He regretted, however, that the call for immediate action made by Ms. Machel had gone largely unheeded. More concrete things had to be done, not least to give children a voice in resolving conflict. "Whatever your ideas are, you haven't done very well with them", he told representatives in the unusually crowded conference room. In a question and answer session, he went on to stress the importance of conflict prevention, saying that in the past decade, he had become aware of a pattern of reluctance and lack of political will to respond to conflict situations at their very early stages.

"Sometimes children were the intended targets, and not just caught in the cross fire."

The Committee also heard from Radhika Coomaraswamy, Special Representative of the Secretary-General for Children and Armed Conflict, who drew attention to the forthcoming strategic review of the Machel study. She reported that in the past year, progress had been made on action plans to end the recruitment of children by armed forces. Reintegration processes for released children, however, now had to be strengthened. She also called for an end to impunity for those who abused and exploited children in conflict situations. And she recalled a boy she had met on a trip to the Middle East, who had asked her why the United Nations talked so much but did so little. "I hope his words will haunt all of us as we try and implement the recommendations of the Machel review," she said.

Speaking before the Committee as well was Ann M. Veneman, Executive Director of the United Nations Children's Fund (UNICEF), who said that the impact of conflict on children was still as brutal as ever. Sometimes children were the intended targets, and not just caught in the cross fire. She too said that children and youth were key to defining their own future, and that their contributions to peacemaking and peacebuilding should not be underestimated. . . .

Portugal's Response

Catarina de Albuquerque, speaking on behalf of the European Union and associated States, said many important achievements and landmarks in the area of children's rights existed, and those should guide the international community in identifying and overcoming unmet challenges. Eighteen years ago, the General Assembly adopted the Convention on the Rights of the Child. It had been ratified more quickly and by more Governments than any other human rights instrument. It had also increasingly been considered in national and international judicial decisions, while having an impact on numerous international legal instruments. In the last 15 years, the Convention's monitoring body, the Committee on the Rights of the Child, had received almost 400 state reports on the application of the Convention and its Optional Protocols.

This year also marked other anniversaries: the fifth anniversary of the Convention's two Optional Protocols on the Involvement of Children in Armed Conflict and on the Sale of Children, Child Prostitution and Child Pornography; the tenth anniversary of Graça Machel's groundbreaking report on the *Impact of Armed Conflict on Children*; and the first year of implementation of recommendations of the United Nations

Study on Violence. A mid-decade review of the United Nations special session on children would also take place this year, she observed.

"It was no longer a question of what was possible, but of priorities."

Despite these achievements, children still faced injustice, violence and exploitation. She said many children—particularly girls, children in rural areas, indigenous children, children of ethnic minorities or migrant children—were still victims of discrimination, poverty and exclusion.

Inspiring examples of children and youth having greater participation in decisions that affected their lives existed, but such participation was rarely built into local practices and national systems. The Convention's normative and ethical framework, the special session on children's issues, and the results of the mid-decade review would be a strong foundation for the future. Children's rights had been placed on the map in the last 18 years, and the coming years would be key to effectively mainstreaming those rights into the national and international agendas and translating them into relevant public policies. It was no longer a question of what was possible, but of priorities.

Namibia's Response

Kaire Munionganda Mbuende, speaking for the Southern African Development Community (SADC), said the overall situation of children in sub-Saharan Africa was a source of major concern. Children had increasingly become victims of violence, including domestic violence, sexual exploitation, trafficking and disappearance. That situation was further compounded by a lack of awareness of children's rights, gender and health issues. The community abhorred violence against women and children and, in the past 10 years, had established and amended various laws that prohibited violence against children. It had also implemented various social and cultural initiatives that helped protect the rights of children.

He said Member States in his region had integrated the commitments of "A World Fit for Children" into their existing national development plans and poverty reduction strategies.

Investment in children was consistent with the MDGs [Millennium Development Goals; eight international development goals the UN plans to achieve by 2015]. Indeed, SADC had already made substantial progress in providing universal primary education to children. Providing equal opportunities for girls and boys remained a challenge, however, and girls continued to be more vulnerable to poverty, hunger, insecurity, sexual exploitation and abuse, and HIV/AIDS. Plans of Action at the national level needed to be better funded for changes to correct that trend.

He said several international and regional conventions and policy guidelines existed to protect the rights of orphans and vulnerable children, but, he would ask Member States, what were the values of good policies and commitments if they were not backed up by allocation and flow of resources to ensure that the rights contained in the various instruments were indeed enjoyed. He said he would urge partners to better support efforts to fight problems like HIV/AIDS which severely affected vulnerable children. Ensuring the sufficient resources were available, including cheaper generic drugs, was a good start towards that end. He expressed support for the creation of a position of Special Representative of the Secretary-General on violence against children. He said SADC would soon table a biennial resolution on the "girl-child", which he hoped would be adopted by consensus.

Barbados's Response

Christopher Hackett, speaking for the Caribbean Community (CARICOM), said that his delegation condemned all forms of violence against children and called on the international community to broadly address the challenges faced by the world's young people in order to effectively address the matter. For its part, the CARICOM region had undertaken several initiatives to strengthen child protection mechanisms. At the national level, the community supported the aims of the Convention on the Rights of the Child and the outcome of the General Assembly's 2001 special session on children. At the same time, the region was aware that poverty, conflict, pandemics such as HIV/AIDS, environmental degradation and natural disasters, which hampered development in many countries, also gravely affected the most vulnerable population: children.

Until the international community resolved structural issues, especially those hindering many States from achieving the MDGs, developing countries would continue to lag behind the rest of the world. Inevitably, he added, children living in developing countries would be among those who suffered most.

He therefore called for speedier implementation of the decisions made by the "G-8" [group of 8 of the world's industrialized democracies that serves as an international forum] countries in 2005 at Gleneagles in Scotland, and at the Assembly's World Summit, to boost development assistance. Such increased official development assistance (ODA) must also be coupled with serious efforts to open world markets to the goods of developing countries. That would also require improved global governance and improved coherence among United Nations agencies. Overall, the voice of the United Nations in the global development policy dialogue should be enhanced.

He said CARICOM had repeatedly drawn attention to the urgent need to tackle the AIDS pandemic; the reality was that despite the general worldwide improvement in child mortality rates, HIV/AIDS had been reversing the progress achieved in

---

The Worldwide Status of Children in Military Schools

States **do not admit** under-18s into military schools	Albania, Bosnia Herzegovina, Cameroon, Croatia, Denmark, Estonia, Jordan, Lebanon, Moldova, Mongolia, Slovenia, Spain, Switzerland, Saudi Arabia, Syria and Tunisia.
States admit under-18s into military schools but students **are not members** of the armed forces	Latvia, Luxembourg, Macedonia, Nepal, New Zealand, Pakistan, Slovakia, Sri Lanka, Sweden and Turkey.
States admit under-18s into military schools and students **are members** of the armed forces	Australia, Azerbaijan, Bangladesh, Belgium, Brunei Darussalam, Canada, China, Eritrea, Cuba, Georgia, India, Israel, Italy, Japan, Kazakhstan, Kyrgyzstan, Mexico, Myanmar, Netherlands, North Korea, The Philippines, Portugal, Romania, Russia, Singapore, United Kingdom, [United States], Viet Nam.

TAKEN FROM: "Submission to the UN Study on Violence Against Children, with Specific Reference to Children in Military Schools and to Children in Peacetime Government Forces," Coalition to Stop the Use of Child Soldiers, March 2005.

---

many areas. Indeed, for small island developing states, the spectre of HIV/AIDS ravaging the youth population was truly daunting.

While calling on the international community to devote more funds and attention to the issue, he said Governments in the region were devoting whatever resources they could to turning back the scourge. He added that public education programmes had been started across the region with the aid of UNICEF.

Sudan's Response

Abdelhamid Abidin Mohamed said the reports put before the Committee would give focus to the general discussion and lead to worthwhile conclusions. The child summit in 1990 had been a landmark in promoting the rights of children, giving impetus to the children's agenda and various concerns and issues. Several of the MDGs touched upon children's issues.

Regarding a proposal for a Special Representative on violence against children, who would have a four-year mandate, it was important that it be accorded more in-depth study, so as to avoid duplication. An informed decision was needed, not a hasty one.

He said Sudan had adopted a framework document entitled *A Sudan Worthy of Children* that embodied "A World Fit for Children". It reflected the country's commitment to MDGs and to regional and international charters on the status of children. Children's policy in Sudan was supervised by a national council on children's welfare, which reported to the Presidency. A breakthrough consolidated law on children was introduced in 2004, and a Children's Parliament convened annually. In Darfur, it was hoped that the peace process would soon be completed. Sudan had grave concerns about Arab children living under occupation in Palestine and the Syrian Golan; it called upon the international community to resolve that problem.

Sri Lanka's Response

Mahinda Samarasinghe, Minister of Disaster Management and Human Rights of Sri Lanka, said sound social policies and legal measures had already been introduced nationally to promote and protect the rights of children. Consistent investment in universal access to education, from primary school to university, had resulted in high rates of enrolment and literacy, and his country was now on track to meet MDGs for primary education, school gender parity and reproductive health services. Child and maternal mortality had been reduced to levels that were comparable with those in some developed countries, and an effective public health system combined with a system of free education was resulting in considerable progress in social development.

However, he said, despite significant success in improving the lives of children, his Government's achievements had been undermined by the forced recruitment of children by a terrorist group which had been banned by several Member States. All possible measures to stop those actions had been taken, but terrorist groups continued to recruit children and had yet to release some still in their custody, despite promises to the contrary.

"Children were the most vulnerable of all those affected by prolonged armed conflict and poverty, and adults were responsible for creating a world fit for their future."

He said Sri Lanka's strict legal framework to protect children from forced recruitment was ineffective against terrorist groups that functioned outside that framework and in blatant disregard of national and international norms. He said he called on the international community to initiate a process to stop the recruitment of children for use in armed conflict, and to help national initiatives to rehabilitate and reintegrate children released by terrorist groups. Doing so would guarantee the protection of all children from all forms of violence and exploitation, wherever they might occur.

Japan's Response

Nobuko Kurosaki said that as a paediatric surgeon who has practised for more than 20 years, he told the Committee that the children he had treated had struggled, not only for their health, but because of prejudice caused by some people's misunderstandings of illness. Children were the most vulnerable of all those affected by prolonged armed conflict and poverty, and adults were responsible for creating a world fit for their future.

As a State party to the Convention on the Rights of the Child, he said Japan had made both domestic and international efforts to promote and protect children's rights. To combat child abuse, one of the most serious human rights problems today, Japan had revised its child abuse prevention law and child welfare laws. Those revisions were meant to strengthen the role of child guidance centres and to introduce a new system to confirm safe conditions for children. Along with other Member States, Japan had also given assistance totalling about 2.2 million U.S. dollars, through the [United Nations] Trust Fund for Human Security, to the project entitled "Basic Education/Literacy, Income Security and Employment for Vulnerable People Including Children and Women in Bhutan".

He commended UNICEF's follow-up to the Secretary-General's study on violence against children, presented last year, by providing technical support to countries implementing the study's recommendations. He also welcomed UNICEF's latest study on the issue of violence by Mr. Paulo Pinheiro and urged the agency to continue its valuable work to effectively implement the recommendations contained in that report.

Although progress had been made on the issue of children and armed conflict such as the application of international standards for the protection of children, he said there was still much to be done. He stressed that the issue should be a priority for the international community and should be mainstreamed into all policies and programmes of the United Nations. Japan would participate in the high-level plenary meeting on 11 and 12 December of this year [2007] to mark the passing of half a decade since the convening of the special session of the Assembly on children. That meeting would afford a review of the implementation of the Declaration and Plan of Action and provide an opportunity to renew the determination to achieve the goal of creating a "World Fit for Children".

Africa Must Stop Recruiting Children to War

Ernest Harsch

In the following viewpoint, Ernest Harsch provides details about the "Free Children from War" conference held in Paris, France, in February 2007. At the conference, numerous countries that have been home to child soldiers signed on to a campaign to end the recruitment of child soldiers. Although the signatures indicated nothing legally binding, they indicated hope for the future. Harsch quotes former child soldier Ishmael Beah, who stated that although children fight in wars, none of them were born violent. Harsch is a journalist and the managing editor of Africa Renewal.

As you read, consider the following questions:

1. Who is Ishmael Beah and why is he quoted in this article?
2. What was the purpose of the Free Children from War conference?
3. Why did the conference single out the difficulties involving girl soldiers?

Governments and armed groups that recruit children into their military ranks should no longer be allowed to "slip through the net," French Foreign Minister Philippe Douste-

Ernest Harsch, "Pact to End Use of Children in War," *Africa Renewal*, vol. 21, no. 1, April 2007, pp. 4–6. Reproduced by permission.

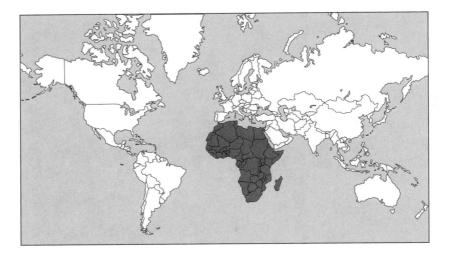

Blazy told a 5–6 February [2007] conference in Paris. He warned that such "lost children" represent a time bomb that could threaten stability and growth in Africa and beyond.

Mr. Ishmael Beah, a former child soldier from Sierra Leone, elaborated. If young ex-combatants are not rehabilitated, he said, they are at risk of becoming mercenaries. "They know how to use a gun. [If] there is a conflict next door offering $100 a day and all you can loot, they will go back to that." While rehabilitating child soldiers is not easy, he cited his own experience: "I'm living proof that it is possible."

Called the "Free Children from War" conference, the event was organized by the French government and the UN Children's Fund (UNICEF). Fifty-eight governments and dozens of nongovernmental organizations (NGOs) signed a set of principles known as the Paris Commitments, in which they vowed to "spare no effort to end the unlawful recruitment or use of children by armed forces or groups in all regions of the world."

The UN estimates that about 300,000 children (defined as those under 18 years of age) are currently engaged in military conflicts in a score of countries, nearly half of them in Africa. While the Paris Commitments are not legally binding, they do carry significant moral and political weight, conference participants noted. Foreign Minister Youssouf Bakayoko of Côte d'Ivoire called the agreement a "breakthrough."

State Responsibilities

Ever since 1996, when Ms. Graça Machel, Mozambique's former minister of education, submitted a major UN-commissioned report on the impact of conflict on children to the General Assembly, much of the campaign against recruiting child soldiers has been waged by the UN and NGOs.

But in Paris, for the first time, numerous governments signed on to that effort, including a number from countries where significant numbers of children still serve in military forces. The African signers, for example, included Burundi, Chad, Côte d'Ivoire, the Democratic Republic of the Congo, Somalia, Sudan and Uganda.

"Child soldiers who have committed crimes should not be regarded only as perpetrators, but 'primarily as victims of violations against international law.'"

"States bear the primary responsibility" for protecting children and reintegrating them into civilian life, argues the Paris Commitments document. Concretely, doing that includes identifying and securing the release of all children recruited by armed groups, "unconditionally at all times, including during armed conflict." In other words, the act of freeing children from military service should not be dependent on a cease-fire or peace agreement, nor should armed groups be allowed to use the presence of children in their ranks to gain leverage in peace negotiations.

In addition, states the document, peace agreements must not grant amnesty to commanders or others who have recruited or committed other crimes against children. Governments and courts must seek to prosecute those guilty of such

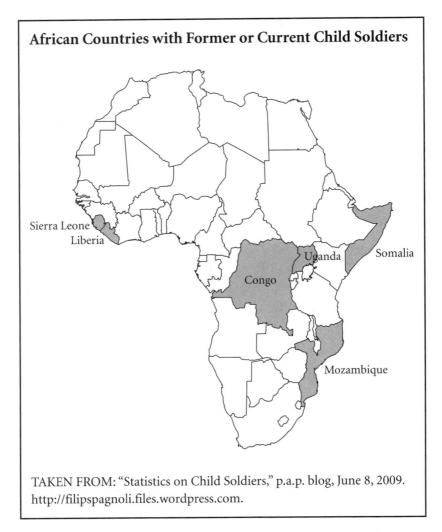

African Countries with Former or Current Child Soldiers

Sierra Leone
Liberia

Uganda
Somalia

Congo

Mozambique

TAKEN FROM: "Statistics on Child Soldiers," p.a.p. blog, June 8, 2009.
http://filipspagnoli.files.wordpress.com.

acts. Encouraging such efforts, the International Criminal Court announced just a week before the Paris conference that it was opening its first trial, that of a militia leader from the eastern DRC [Democratic Republic of the Congo] accused of recruiting child soldiers.

Meanwhile, the conference participants agreed, child soldiers who have committed crimes should not be regarded only as perpetrators, but "primarily as victims of violations against international law." In line with international standards for juvenile justice, authorities should seek alternatives to judicial proceedings.

Attention to Girls

The conference singled out the plight of girls, many of whom have been abducted by fighting forces to serve as domestic slaves, and who suffer rape and other sexual abuse and sometimes are compelled to fight. In some groups, girls make up 40 percent of the children recruited, according to UN estimates.

"Girls in particular are forced to perform sexual services," noted UNICEF Executive Director Ann Veneman. As a result, she added, they are deprived of "their rights and their childhood." The Paris Commitments call on governments and other actors to "meet the specific needs of girls and their children for protection and assistance."

"While some children may 'voluntarily' join an armed group—usually to obtain food or protection—'no one is born violent.'"

For both girls and boys who have been freed from military service, long-term support is essential for their rehabilitation and reintegration, conference participants emphasized. Poor African countries often lack the resources to carry out the task on their own. "We are calling on the international community to assist us in reintegrating the child soldiers into society," appealed Ms. Qamar Aden, president of Somalia's parliamentary human rights committee. She estimated that some 70,000 children have been recruited by all sides in Somalia's most recent conflict.

While some children may "voluntarily" join an armed group—usually to obtain food or protection—"no one is born violent," Mr. Beah noted in Paris. "No child in Africa, Latin America or Asia wants to be part of war."

British Relief Organization Offers Aid to Children Affected by War in Sierra Leone

Lindsay Clydesdale

In the following viewpoint, Lindsay Clydesdale laments over the plight of war-ravaged children from Sierra Leone. Many children were killed while others were left mutilated and emotionally damaged. In total, the war that lasted from 1991 to 2002 left fifty thousand dead, one hundred thousand mutilated and six thousand abducted (of whom thirty-five hundred fought in the war). Clydesdale wrote three years after peace was restored, but she noted that the scars of war were still present, especially in the children. To help in the healing process, the British charity organization Comic Relief offered funds and other assistance. Clydesdale is a journalist and a lifestyle columnist for the Daily Record.

As you read, consider the following questions:

1. Why, according to the article, were the AK-47 automatic rifle and rocket-propelled grenade launcher suddenly in high demand in Sierra Leone?

2. What kinds of services is Comic Relief providing to residents of Sierra Leone?

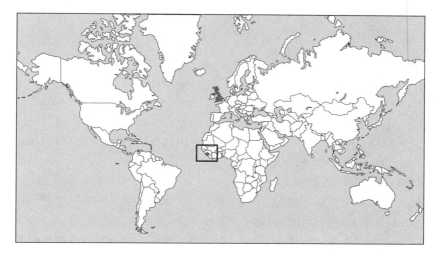

3. Why does the author say that in Sierra Leone "curiosity can be a killer"?

The boy offering help outside the airport seemed no different from the other youngsters milling around. But only minutes after stepping off the plane at Sierra Leone's Lunghi air terminal, I caught my first glimpse of the shocking human cost of war. As the boy moved away from his friends, I saw that both of his hands had been cut off at the wrists. This brutal treatment was dealt out to thousands of innocent children during the country's civil war, for no other reason than to instill fear. The terror tactics by rebels of the Revolutionary United Front [RUF] worked, but sending the nation's youngsters into hiding wasn't enough. Forces on both sides of the war rounded up children from the towns and villages they had plundered and forced them to fight.

Now, three years after peace was restored, almost every child has memories of the war which started in 1991 and left 50,000 people dead and 100,000 mutilated. For an entire generation, normal life means fear, hunger, violence and loss—and these are the lucky ones who survived. Humanitarian programmes to reunite children with their relatives have been under way for some time. But this is no easy task and many child soldiers have had to come to terms with the atrocities they were forced to commit, often against their own communities.

Palm wine, amphetamines and cocaine were used to drug the youngsters before they were sent to fight. An estimated 6,000 were abducted, 3,500 of whom fought. The others were kept as sex slaves. And while the rebels were carrying out the atrocities, the government also swelled its forces with children. One quarter of their fighters were under 18. Weapons such as the AK-47 automatic rifle and rocket-propelled grenade launcher were suddenly in high demand because they were light and easy to wield by 12-year-olds. Others as young as five carried supplies.

"Forces on both sides of the war rounded up children from the towns and villages they had plundered and forced them to fight."

Comic Relief Offers Help

Now child and adult soldiers are being encouraged back into their communities. These former fighters are counselled alongside the victims they terrorised. The people who have suffered so much seem eager to put those evil days behind them and focus on rebuilding the country. At a project launched last month in Bandawor, MAPCO (Movement for Assistance and Promotion of Rural Communities) is using Comic Relief [a British charity organization] funds to run training in gardening, food management and making clothes. Counselling forms part of the programme, a necessity for the children who, even if they weren't victims, witnessed murder, rape, torture and forced amputation.

Project manager Francis Lavally said: 'The re-integration of ex-combatants into the village has been very effective. Counselling is worked into the day alongside training classes in soap making, sewing and blacksmithing. It has not been easy, but there is a real sense of pulling together and putting the conflict behind us. If the men are given other ways to live, they won't so easily turn to violence again. All the people, children in particular, need projects and work to distract them from their memories of the horrors of the war.'

Helping these children and young adults believe there is a future worth living for is a central theme of the projects Comic Relief fund[s] in Sierra Leone. Giving hope to this generation is vital to preventing civil war born of poverty and despair erupting again. There are constant reminders of the blood that's been shed—the pointless destruction of homes, schools and buildings and the lack of teachers, doctors and nurses. Education is one of the Sierra Leone government's priorities and around half of their primary schools are now operating, albeit in inadequate conditions. But while primary education is free, secondary school comes with charges for books, equipment and enrolment. This prevents most children from attending.

"It has not been easy, but there is a real sense of pulling together and putting the conflict behind us."

The Children Must Fight for Life

In Bandawor, where the children live in the shadows of broken-down, bullet-ridden buildings, the damage caused by the war is still clear to see. Curiosity in this country can be a killer and posters in Senehun warn kids not to go near unexploded shells. But many need look no further than their own bodies for the destruction of war. When rebels attacked villages, adults fled, sometimes leaving children behind, believing they would not be harmed. But the heartless rebels chopped off the kids' hands with machetes.

Kula Mansaray was 15 when her community in Kenema was attacked. She hid in the bush for three months, separated

---

Statistics on Child Labor in Sierra Leone

- More than 10,000 children in the country have been serving as child soldiers with the rebels and civil militia.

- The percentage of child soldiers is perhaps over 50%.

- Some 5,000 child combatants serve among government and opposition forces, and a further 5,000 are estimated to have been recruited for labour among armed groups.

- It has been estimated than one third of all underage soldiers are girls.

Global March,
"Worst Forms of Child Labor Data."
www.globalmarch.org.

---

from her family, before making her way in desperation to a refugee camp. She stayed there for three years until 1997 when, despite the danger, she decided to go home. 'I wanted to be back in a place that I knew and be with my family, my community,' she said. 'But when I returned, our belongings were gone. Our house was destroyed, as were all the others in the village. So I had to make a mud hut and that's what we live in to this day.' But it wasn't just her home the rebels had destroyed. Her sister and grandfather were killed in a gunfight. 'They were caught by stray bullets when the rebels attacked,' said Kula. Now married with two children, Kula is keen to have some independence and is learning to make soap in the MAPCO project.

Even without the atrocities of war, the children have to fight for life from the day they are born. One quarter of all children in Sierra Leone will die before the age of five. Counsellor Ansumara Sheriff says the biggest problem is a lack of food. 'We are always hungry,' he said. 'We don't have enough food from farming to last the year. So the majority of the children have just one meal a day, in the evening, and go to school or do their chores on an empty stomach.'

Christian Aid project worker Gaspard Ngevao lost his mother during the war, but has focussed his grief on helping children through his project, the Association for People's Empowerment. His mother was shot then set on fire by the rebels.

Gaspard said: 'It's hard to talk about the war because of what happened to my mother, but I was born poor and struggled to live every day. I will fight for the rest of my life to make sure no other child has to go through that again.'

With Comic Relief donations, Gaspard may well get that wish.

In Mozambique, Save the Children Helps Child Soldiers Heal

Wray Herbert

In the following viewpoint, Wray Herbert discusses the challenges that former child soldiers face in Mozambique and investigates why some former child soldiers cope better than others. Herbert says the following aided in recovery: a nurturing orphanage called Lhanguene; the relief organization Save the Children; and close family ties. Still, it is important to remember that "success" for Mozambique's former child soldiers is very different from Western interpretations of success. Herbert is a journalist who has been writing about psychology and human behavior for over 25 years. He currently writes the We're Only Human blog for Newsweek.

As you read, consider the following questions:

1. How long did Mozambique's civil war last?
2. How did the interventions at Lhanguene help former child soldiers to heal?
3. What are the differences and similarities in diagnosis and healing between Mozambique and Western cultures?

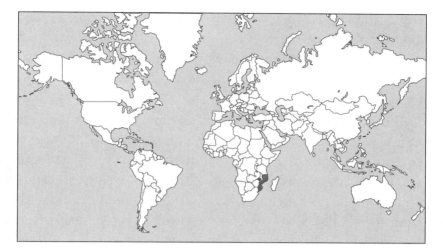

Alfredo Betuel Macamo and Joaquim Fernando Quive live only a couple of hundred yards from each other, and they share a lot of history and culture. These two 23-year-old men grew up in the same primitive village near Malehice in the rural Mozambican province of Gaza, and both still live there today. It's a poor place, and neither Macamo nor Quive is doing that great financially. Macamo is struggling to raise three kids—6, 3, and a 4-month-old—by harvesting reeds on a riverbank. Quive does odd jobs when he can find them, though these days he doesn't work much at all. They both live in small reed huts with dirt floors and no running water.

Despite all they have in common, Macamo and Quire are worlds apart psychologically and socially. When I visited Macamo recently, I was greeted not only by him but by 12 members of his extended family, all decked out in traditional African garb. We sat around in plastic chairs, the kind you buy at Kmart, or on mats under the mafureira tree that is the center of their yard, and talked about Macamo's life, past and present. It was celebratory.

Quive's home is a lonelier place. It has two huts, but the larger of the two—his father's—sits empty. His father has been expelled from the village for stealing a radio. Quive occupies the smaller hut in a grim, empty yard. He doesn't have any chairs, but he borrows a couple of the Kmart chairs from a neighbor and lays out a reed mat for a visitor. Quive has also dressed up, in a silky white shirt. But there's no family here, just Quive.

I'm talking to Macamo and Quive, and other young men in a few villages nearby, because of something they all have in common. During the 16-year civil war that devastated this sprawling coastal nation in southeastern Africa, Macamo, Quive, and their neighbors were all child soldiers, abducted from their villages as kids and taken to distant camps run by the rebel forces trying to topple the government at the time. All, eventually, escaped and through circuitous routes ended up in the Lhanguene orphanage in Maputo, the capital city to the south. All the boys were eventually reunited with their families in their natal villages, and that's where most live today. And there the commonalities end.

U.S. News [& World Report] first reported on these child soldiers in 1989, when the war was still raging. The purpose of my trip to this beautiful but primitive region of Africa was to revisit the child soldiers 15 years later, to see how they are doing now that the civil war is over and they have resumed something like a normal life. Most, like Macamo and Quive, are men now. Some, like Macamo, are raising kids of their own. All suffer to some degree from their abductions and their experience of war as children. Some are doing better than others.

Soldiers and Spies

Mozambique has not known much other than war since the mid-1960s; until the 1990s, many Mozambicans grew up not knowing what peace looked like. First, there was the 10-year revolutionary war to oust the Portuguese, who had colonized the country in the 1500s and ruled it for more than four centuries. The Portuguese were finally challenged by the Mozambique Liberation Front, or Frelimo, the Marxist insurgency that ousted the colonizers in 1975. But as soon as Frelimo prevailed and the Portuguese fled, the new Frelimo government faced an insurgency of its own, financed mostly by what was then the neighboring nation of Rhodesia and later by South Africa. The guerrillas, known as the Mozambique National Resistance, or Renamo, were based mostly in the rural north. They had no particular ideology, other than their desire to oust Frelimo.

That's where the child soldiers came in. The Renamo leaders began recruiting from rural villages, and if they couldn't recruit able-bodied young boys, they simply kidnapped them. Most of the recruits were 12, 13, 14 years old, but some were as young as 6. The youngest boys often served as porters and servants to Renamo officers, or as spies, but most were systematically trained to be soldiers. They were exposed to the noise of rifle blasts, to desensitize them. They were ordered to kill cattle; then, when they got used to that, to kill other humans, often those who ignored orders or tried to escape. The perimeters of the rebels' camps were often littered with the skulls of those who had tried to escape but failed.

It is remarkable, given all of the terrorist indoctrination, that Renamo converted so few of the kids it captured. Perhaps because Renamo stood for nothing, perhaps because its soldiers were so brutal, it appears that most of the child soldiers in its ragtag ranks never stopped thinking of themselves as captives or victims. Some certainly "went Renamo" out of self-preservation, and some even liked their newfound power as warriors, but most kept their minds focused on finding a chance to escape.

Inevitably, given Renamo's obvious lack of soldierly deportment and order, the opportunities eventually presented themselves. Rafael Vicente Saveca's chance came when his camp was switching locations. Rafael was sent by Renamo officers to fetch water. He seized the chance to flee, hiding in huts in friendly villages before finally returning to his village, near Chibuto. To avoid recapture, or worse, Rafael disappeared, wandering for months, until Frelimo soldiers finally detained him in a prisoner-of-war camp.

"Most of the recruits were 12, 13, 14 years old, but some were as young as 6."

A Safe Haven for Kids

A lot of Mozambican boys like Rafael had similar experiences. The Renamo camps were heavily policed, but the boys managed to escape during battles or while on missions to gather wood or hunt for food. Then, often, they would vanish into the bush, moving from village to village at night, resting and hiding during the day. The stretch of bush between Maputo and Gaza is pretty desolate even today. Back in the late 1980s it was salted with land mines, almost constantly policed by government and guerrilla troops.

Like Rafael, many of Renamo's child soldiers ended up in Frelimo jails before they were transferred to the Lhanguene orphanage in Maputo. Orphanage, actually, is something of a misnomer. The kids at Lhanguene came from such tightly knit, extended families that their language hardly distinguished between father and uncle, sibling or cousin. With such large families, and such tight bonds among members, the true orphan at Lhanguene was rare. But calling Lhanguene an orphanage had public relations value for the Frelimo government, because it was a visible reminder of Renamo's brutality toward Mozambique's children. Whatever its significance to the larger world, Lhanguene was a safe haven for the kids lucky enough to find their way there—and the first step on their uncertain journey of healing.

There were thousands of boys abducted by Renamo and forced to train as soldiers. Some were with the rebel forces just months, others for as long as three years. The person who has treated and studied these kids most intensely is psychologist Neil Boothby. Now a professor of public health at Columbia University, Boothby at the time worked for Save the Children, the international aid organization that works to assist kids around the globe whose lives have been disrupted by war, including the deslocados who ended up at the Lhanguene orphanage.

"Boys managed to escape during battles or while on missions to gather wood or hunt for food."

Mechanisms for Healing

The interventions at Lhanguene were deceptively simple. Indeed, when I asked the men about their time at Lhanguene, without exception the first thing they mentioned was playing soccer. At first I just noted this and dismissed it as a childish memory, but when it came up again and again I began to realize that soccer wasn't trivial to these child soldiers' psychological recovery. What they wanted more than anything—and Boothby's later research with many other child soldiers documented this—was to once again be "like everyone else." Playing soccer did a lot of things—it reestablished rules and sense of fair play—but perhaps most important, it made them feel "normal" in their own minds. In psychological jargon, they were moving from a survival mentality, which they had adopted of necessity, to a security mentality normal for their age. In other words, they were learning to become kids again.

Other interventions more directly involved resolving the wartime traumas of these children. They were encouraged, for example, to draw pictures, and when they did their drawings included typical childhood things like houses and family—but they also included, often tucked off in a corner, an automatic weapon, a slain body. Such drawings provided an opening for discussion about the horrific experiences they were reluctant to bring up themselves. So did the use of psychodramas, which were explicit opportunities for the kids to act out, and denounce, the hateful acts of Renamo, and in addition to celebrate the virtues of nation, community, and family.

I asked Boothby at one point if there was a clear greatest success story among the kids with whom he worked to heal and reconnect with their homes and families. He explained that there are three dimensions that define success and failure for these young men: financial success, marital stability, and the classical measures of mental health like clear thinking and emotional steadiness.

"What they wanted more than anything . . . was to once again be 'like everyone else.'"

If you're talking about traditional Western ideals of career and financial success, almost none of these former child soldiers could be called successful. One, Angelo Jose Macouvele, went on to become a professional photographer, working both in Mozambique and in the much more affluent South Africa. But he is the exception. Most are subsistence farmers, raising maize and beans to feed their own families, then looking for real currency income where they can find it.

Child Soldiers Lost Prime Earning Years

Take the case of Israel Armando Massingue, who was abducted by Renamo in 1987, when he was 14 years old; he's in his early 30s today. He dresses in Western clothes including an "America on the Rise" T-shirt. He is handsome and fit like a college running back, with an engaging smile. He is the president of the local equivalent of the PTA. His wife, Sangina Salvador Sitoe, attests that he is a good husband: He doesn't drink and he isn't rough with me, she says.

Yet Massingue cannot find work. He raises his food crops right now, but he is more ambitious than that and feels he

Save the Children's Interventions in Mozambique Included

- strengthening children's coping skills for trauma and grief,

- undoing the harsh and violent indoctrination imposed by the guerrillas,

- promoting appropriate behaviors for civilian life,

- teaching job skills through apprenticeships,

- tracing family ties,

- enlisting local healers to perform "cleansing ceremonies," and

- conducting community sensitization campaigns to encourage communities to help rehabilitate children once they returned home.

Save the Children, "Success Story: Mozambique's Child Soldiers: What Happened to Mozambique's Lost Generation of Children?" www.savethechildren.org.

just needs a leg up to start some sort of small business. He dreams of getting a small piece of property where he could build a furnace, and produce concrete blocks for construction, or perhaps have a small chicken farm. But such dreams are a long shot.

Massingue is representative of how these young men were often financially crippled by their abductions and forced servitude in the Renamo forces. Typically, teenagers from rural Mozambique will venture away from home for a few years, often to South Africa to work in the mines, and earn enough money to return home with a financial stake. They use their savings to attract a bride, they marry, and raise families. These young men never got to South Africa and lost those prime earning years.

They also lost their chances for a decent education. Basic education is not an entitlement in Mozambique; the cost of textbooks alone makes schooling prohibitively expensive for many, especially those in rural areas. Yet most of the boys from Lhanguene, who were all offered stipends to resume their education once they were back home, turned them down. They wanted to make up for lost time, to get on with the lives that had been interrupted. So Macamo, who had gotten only to fourth grade, never resumed his schooling. Massingue did try to go back to school, but then he was drafted into the Frelimo Army and lost even more time. Now in his 30s, he sees education as a luxury he can't afford to indulge.

"He dreams of getting a small piece of property. . . . But such dreams are a long shot."

A Different Measure for Success

Yet despite their poor financial fortunes, many are married and raising families. By that measure, Boothby notes, most would be considered successes, though raising families in such abject poverty is tough. Massingue and Sitoe's infant daughter had died just days before I visited, the second of their two children to die. The cause of death isn't known. Macamo has also lost one child. Losing children is not uncommon in rural Mozambique.

Despite such losses and the accompanying grief, Massingue and Macamo would have to be considered successes in terms of social functioning. Certainly compared with Firinice Nharala. Firinice was only 6 when he was abducted by Renamo and witnessed the brutal murder of family members who were Frelimo supporters. When he ended up at Lhanguene, he was mute, and although he later regained his voice, he was by all reports never completely healthy again. He was delusional much of the time, and in his early 20s he was still living in the care of his mother. That is where I was supposed to meet him, but I never got the chance. Ten days before I arrived in Mozambique, Nharala drowned in a nearby lake while fishing.

Quive is another who never really recovered from his wartime experience. He has never married, and his prospects aren't very good. The fact is he doesn't have much to offer. His teeth are rotten, and he has no income. Indeed, he represents the walking wounded of the children's civil war. He spent two years in a Renamo base camp, working as a colonel's bodyguard. In that role, he would have both witnessed and committed some brutal acts. He says he still has nightmares and flashbacks about his time with Renamo, sometimes so disabling that they keep him from doing even the simplest work. One day, while cutting wood with a machete, he had flashbacks so severe that he nearly severed his arm, and he hasn't worked much since. If he were in America, he would most likely be diagnosed with post-traumatic stress disorder, or PTSD, and treated with psychotherapeutic techniques and perhaps psychiatric medications.

Stress and Culture

Diagnosis and healing in Mozambique are very different from Western practices, but there are interesting commonalities as well. I spent some time talking to traditional healers, known locally as curandeiros: Rosalina Mondlane and Teresa Xitlango live and work in the same Malehice village as Macamo and Quive. Beatriz Armando Massingue lives in Israel's village; she's his sister. These women are highly regarded in their communities. They have all apprenticed to other healers for three to five years, and although the specifics of their healing practices appear to vary a bit, they all share some general beliefs about mental health and psychotherapy.

They wouldn't use those words, of course, though when pushed they do come up with words for conditions that are roughly translatable to our psychiatric diagnoses. For example, the Shangana word kuxukuvala is a close equivalent of what we would call clinical depression. Kuxukuvala is characterized by abnormal sadness and emotional paralysis. Similarly, Quive and others are thought to suffer from npfuka, which corresponds pretty well to what American psychiatrists would label PTSD. It has the symptoms of nightmares and flashbacks to specific experiences of trauma and violence.

"Most of the kids were welcomed back with compassion, even joy, and the healers' belief in recovery certainly helped the communities embrace their victimized sons."

But the Mozambican healers' theories about the causes of such stress disorders are quite different. They believe, for example, that when a soldier murders someone, the spirit of the dead takes up residence in the killer—even if the murder has been coerced, as with the child soldiers. For the sake of mental stability, the spirit of the victim must be driven out.

To that end, the healers might heat a concoction of local herbs and have the returning soldiers breathe it in to accomplish spiritual cleansing. Or they might kill a chicken or a goat, mix the blood with water, then use this potion to "vaccinate" them through pinpricks in the arm. If the healers sense the need for a stronger treatment, they might take the child down to the riverside, because certain spirits are known to reside in the water or in the riverbanks and exposure to these spirits can be tonic. All of this must be done before the emotionally traumatized child is allowed to reenter the household, to prevent contamination of the home. The healers appear to have an innate sense of what American mental health practitioners call psychiatric prevention; they assume that such trauma and stress will take a toll even if it hasn't already, so they intervene immediately to ward off illness by maligning the spirits.

It's impossible to know which specific elements of these healing practices helped the returning child soldiers, but it's clear that the cleansing rituals were essential to the kids' transitions back to community and family life. When the civil war came to an end, there was a widespread fear that the boys who had served under Renamo would be socially tainted and unwelcome back in their villages because of their "treason" and the hideousness of their war crimes. Indeed, this idea was perpetuated by the Frelimo government, which saw PR value in the idea that Renamo had ruined these kids' lives. But the rejections never happened. Most of the kids were welcomed back with compassion, even joy, and the healers' belief in recovery certainly helped the communities embrace their victimized sons.

Back Home

So why have some done so much better after the war than others? Put another way, why aren't all of the former child soldiers psychological wrecks given what they were put through? The answer is no doubt complex, but at least two factors appear important to the survivors' resilience. The first is the amount of time the child spent with Renamo. Some, like Macamo and Rafael Saveca, escaped after just a couple of months, while others, like Quive, were in Renamo camps for two years or more. According to Boothby's analysis, there is an emotional "threshold" somewhere between months and years. Once passed, it's much harder to repair the psychological damage.

Then there is family. All of these kids got basically the same psychological help at Lhanguene, and almost all went through some kind of cleansing ritual upon returning to their villages. But Macamo and Massingue came home to large, exuberant families. Quive, by contrast, came home to a disintegrating household. His parents had split up while he was gone, and when he sided with his mother, his father disowned him. The village healers, Mondlane and Xitlango, say Quive's mother is unstable; they use a Shangana word that roughly translates as "she sleeps around." Indeed, she and her latest boyfriend left the village soon after Quive returned.

So Quive has not had much emotional support at home. But consider that he is one of the lucky child soldiers. He at least ended up at Lhanguene, where he benefited from Save the Children's model therapy program. When the civil war ended in 1992, both Frelimo and Renamo denied ever enlisting children in their war efforts, so about 25,000 kids were left to reintegrate themselves into their communities without any help whatsoever. Those young men's life stories are not known.

Despite International Efforts, Child Soldiers Continue to Be Used in Battle

Coalition to Stop the Use of Child Soldiers

In the following viewpoint, the Coalition to Stop the Use of Child Soldiers stresses that the international community must do more to combat the use of child soldiers. Although some progress has been made, child soldiers continue to be used throughout the world by governments and armed groups. In addition to ceasing the use of children in war, former child soldiers need rehabilitation and help with reintegration into society. The Coalition to Stop the Use of Child Soldiers works to prevent the recruitment of child soldiers, to demobilize them, and to help them rehabilitate and reintegrate into society.

As you read, consider the following questions:

1. According to the *Child Soldiers Global Report 2008*, by how much has the number of armed conflicts involving children decreased between 2004 and 2007?
2. Which country has most persistently continued to use child soldiers?
3. When it comes to the reintegration of child soldiers, how are girls rendered more invisible than boys?

Coalition to Stop the Use of Child Soldiers, "Media Statement: International Efforts Still Failing Child Soldiers," Child Soldiers Global Report 2008, www.childsoldiers globalreport.org, May 20, 2008. Reproduced by permission.

Despite progress, efforts to end the recruitment and use of child soldiers are too little and too late for many children, according to the *Child Soldiers Global Report 2008*, launched today by the Coalition to Stop the Use of Child Soldiers.

The report details how a near global consensus that children should not be used as soldiers, and strenuous international efforts—with the UN at the forefront—to halt the phenomenon, have failed to protect tens of thousands of children from war. When armed conflict exists, children will almost inevitably become involved as soldiers.

The report documents military recruitment legislation, policy and practice in more than 190 countries worldwide—in conflict and in peacetime armies—as well as child soldier use by non-state armed groups.

"The international community's commitment to ending the global scourge of child soldiering cannot be doubted, but existing efforts are falling short," said Dr. Victoria Forbes Adam, director of the Coalition to Stop the Use of Child Soldiers. "Laws, policies and practices must now be translated into real change to keep children out of armed conflict once and for all."

There have been positive developments over the past four years. The coalition's research shows that the number of armed conflicts in which children are involved is down from 27 in 2004 to 17 by the end of 2007. Tens of thousands of children have been released in that time from armies and armed groups as long-running conflicts in sub-Saharan Africa and elsewhere have ended.

But the report shows that tens of thousands of children remain in the ranks of non-state armed groups in at least 24 different countries or territories. The record of governments is also little improved—children were deployed in armed conflicts by government forces in nine situations of armed conflict, down only one from the 10 such situations recorded when the last *Global Report* was published in 2004.

"Existing strategies have not had the desired impact," said Forbes Adam. "If further progress is to be made, it must be recognized that child soldiers are not only an issue for child rights specialists, but should be on the agendas of all those involved in conflict prevention and resolution, peace-building and development."

"In some countries child soldiers who have escaped, surrendered, or been captured by government forces were locked up instead of receiving support to return to their families and communities."

Children Recruited by Governments and Armed Groups

Myanmar remained the most persistent government offender. Its armed forces, engaged in long-running counter-insurgency operations against a range of ethnic armed groups, still contained thousands of children, some as young as 11 years old. Children were also used by government forces in Chad, the Democratic Republic of the Congo, Somalia, Sudan, Uganda, and Yemen. Palestinian children were used on several occasions as human shields by the Israel Defense Forces, and a few British under-18s were deployed to Iraq up to mid-2005.

The failure of governments to adhere to their international obligations does not end there. In at least 14 countries children have been recruited into auxiliary forces linked to national armies, local civilian defense groups created to support counter-insurgency operations, or by illegal militias and armed groups used as proxies by national armies.

Children have also been used as spies. In some countries child soldiers who have escaped, surrendered, or been captured by government forces were locked up instead of receiving support to return to their families and communities. Burundi, Israel, and the United States were among the countries where there were allegations of ill-treatment or torture of child detainees alleged to have been associated with armed groups.

"Given government obligations to protect children from involvement in armed conflict, there can be no excuse for the armed forces of any country unlawfully using children for military purposes or for committing other human rights violations against them," said Forbes Adam.

Children have also been used in combat by armed groups in at least 18 countries or territories. These children, some 12 years old or even younger, were exposed to death, injury, and psychological trauma. In Afghanistan, Iraq, the occupied Palestinian territories, and Pakistan teenagers were used in suicide attacks.

"Armed groups pose the greatest challenge," said Forbes Adam. "International laws have had limited impact in deterring child soldier use by armed groups. Many groups attach little value to international standards and the need to build fighting strength overrides other considerations. This reality must be confronted and new strategies developed."

"Those who lose out most are girls."

Reintegration Is Essential

The coalition's report also highlights that years of accumulated best practice on releasing children from fighting forces and assisting their rehabilitation and reintegration is being overlooked by those involved in designing and implementing disarmament, demobilization, and reintegration (DDR) programs. Sustained funding for the long-term support of former child soldiers is also rarely available. In the Democratic Republic of the Congo, for example, delayed, unpredictable and

The Impact of Armed Conflict on Children

Societal Preconditions	
War propaganda • Dehumanization of enemy • Enhancing hatred and revenge • Black and white & simplified information	Traumatic experiences • Loss and death • Witnessing humiliation • Witnessing violence
Human ideals and world view • Heroism & risk-taking • Endurance & persistency • Youth as a savior of the nation • Own superiority & disdain of others	National survival • Fear of death • Fear of annihilation

Developmental Preconditions	Familial Risk Dynamics
Cognitive processes • Intensified perception of threat & danger • Generalized expectation of others' malevolence • Narrow & biased problem solving strategies Emotional processes • Numbing of feelings • Difficulty to recognize own and others' feelings • Dominance of negative emotions • Biased towards behavioral expression of feelings Physiological changes • Tolerance for violence • Inhibition of aggression	Parent-child relationship • Punitive parenting & disciplining • Impossibility to protect children • Fear disrupting early attachment Child participation in fighting • Early maturation & responsibility • Reversal of roles • Intrusive memories of violence

Societal, developmental, and familial preconditions and risks for aggressive child development in conditions of war and military violence.

TAKEN FROM: Brian K. Barber (ed), *Adolescents and War: How Youth Deal with Political Violence*, Oxford University Press, 2009.

short-term funding, combined with poor planning and mis-management of the DDR program, meant that some 14,000 former child soldiers were excluded from reintegration support.

Those who lose out most are girls. The existence of girls in fighting forces, in combat and non-combat roles and as victims of sexual slavery, rape and other forms of sexual violence, is well known. Yet the overwhelming majority of girl soldiers are not identified by and do not register in official DDR programs. In Liberia, where the DDR program ended in late 2004, only just over a quarter of the 11,000 girls known to have been associated with fighting forces registered in the official DDR program. Here, as elsewhere, thousands of girls returned to their communities informally with their complex medical, psychosocial, and economic needs unmet.

"Tens of thousands of children—particularly girls—are effectively rendered invisible during the demobilization and reintegration process," said Forbes Adam. "It is not that their needs and vulnerabilities are unrecognized—it is simply a failure to apply lessons learned that is failing these children and their futures."

Progress towards a global standard prohibiting the military recruitment or use in hostilities of children is hampered by continued recruitment of under-18s into peacetime armies. At least 63 governments—including the United Kingdom and United States—allow voluntary recruitment of under-18s, despite the age of adulthood being set at 18 in many countries. Young recruits considered too young to vote or buy alcohol are subjected to military discipline, hazardous activity and are vulnerable to abuse. Active targeting of children, often from deprived backgrounds, raises questions on the depth of these governments' commitment to child protection and whether such recruitment can be genuinely voluntary.

"2012 will mark the 10th anniversary of the enactment of the international treaty on child soldiers," said Forbes Adam.

"Over the next four years the international community must make good on its pledge to end the use of children in armed conflict."

Periodical Bibliography

Community Action	"Make Child Soldiers a Top Priority—French Diplomat," October 15, 2007.
Community Action	"UN Sec'y General Wants Action on Child Soldiers," February 20, 2008.
Economist	"More Suspects in Its Sights; The International Criminal Court," May 26, 2007.
Robert Hirschfield	"Jimmie Briggs: America's Voice for the Child Soldier," *National Catholic Reporter*, June 16, 2006.
Mohit Joshi	"Human Rights Watch Urges UN to Step up Efforts to Arrest Kony," TopNews.in, July 15, 2009. www.topnews.in.
Edith M. Lederer	"UN to Name Those That Kill Children in War," Associated Press, August 4, 2009.
Arthur Max	"Ex-Liberian Chief Pushes Back at US Government," Associated Press, August 7, 2009.
Noah Benjamin Novogrodsky	"Challenging Impunity," *New Internationalist*, December 2005.
John T. Rawcliffe	"Child Soldiers: Legal Obligations and U.S. Implementation," *Army Lawyer*, September 2007.
Alex Villarrea	"American Youth Rally for Child Soldiers in Uganda's Lord's Resistance Army," *VOA News*, July 16, 2009. www.voanews.com.
Patrick Worsnip	"UN Team to Visit Myanmar over Child Soldiers," Reuters, August 4, 2009. www.reuters.com.
Mu Xuequan	"UN Security Council Acts to Protect Children in War," *China View*, August 5, 2008. www.chinaview.cn.

Life After Combat

Former Cambodian Child Soldier Finds Solace in Writing

Susan Mansfield

In the following viewpoint, Susan Mansfield shares the story of Loung Ung, a former child soldier from Cambodia. When Pol Pot took over her country, Ung's father was killed and Ung, at the age of eight, was trained as a soldier. After the collapse of Pol Pot's regime, Ung was taken to the United States by her brother. But the healing of her past—helped by the writing of her autobiography—would remain a lifetime effort. Mansfield is a journalist for the Scotsman.

As you read, consider the following questions:

1. What was Ung's life like up to the age of five?
2. Why did Ung's brother choose to take her to the United States?
3. What made Ung stop herself from committing suicide?

It's hard to know what to say to Loung Ung. I've been reading about her life, her childhood in the Killing Fields of Cambodia, losing both parents and two of her sisters to Pol Pot's regime. How she trained as a child soldier, endured starvation, forced labour and attempted rape all before the age of ten. Any response sounds like a meaningless platitude.

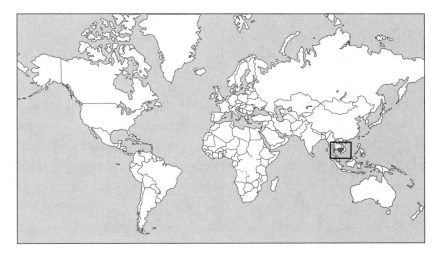

Ung, a petite, beautiful Cambodian American woman of 37, is used to this kind of reaction. "That has been a sad effect of my book (her riveting memoir *First They Killed My Father[: A Daughter of Cambodia Remembers]*). I want people to know that this petite slice of a woman is just like many of your friends. In the last century, 120 million people have survived wars. How many of us are out there?"

It was thinking about the aftermath of war which prompted her to write her second book, *After They Killed Our Father[: A Refugee from the Killing Fields Reunites with the Sister She Left Behind]*, which takes up the story after she arrives in the United States aged ten. Seeing George Bush standing under a "Mission Accomplished" banner three months after invading Iraq, she felt that people needed to be reminded that war is never so simple. "War isn't over just because someone says it is. The process of peace takes many, many years. My first book is about surviving the war, the second is about surviving the peace."

A Horrible Turn of Events

Ung was five, the sixth of seven children, when the Khmer Rouge marched into Phnom Penh in April 1975. The daughter of a high-ranking government official, she led a privileged life with trips to the market, cinema and swimming pool, sneaking off to buy junk food from street vendors when her parents weren't looking.

When Pol Pot's army rolled into the city, evacuating the inhabitants at gunpoint, the Ungs fled, snatching what they could carry and promising their frightened children that they would soon return home. But, reduced to marching for days on end as food supplies dwindled, it became clear there was no going back. Ung remembers being given money by her mother to use as toilet paper—the currency was worthless, the country in free fall.

Living in a succession of jungle villages, starvation and malnutrition threatened as food supplies failed. Ung's elder sister Keav, a beautiful headstrong teenager who had loved clothes and music, died from dysentery because her body was too weak to fight the disease. Ung remembers being so hungry that one night she stole a handful of rice from the family's meagre store. The guilt haunted her for years.

"I think very few Westerners know what it is to be really hungry. In America it's so funny, people flush out their system with colonics and slim ballerina tea. In Cambodia there were times I was so hungry there was not even a grain of rice to line the intestine. A fistful of rice feels like a lifetime of meals."

Always they feared a knock on the door. Pol Pot's bid to create an agrarian utopia saw professional people and former officials slaughtered without mercy. Her father's position with the last government made him—and therefore the whole family—an obvious target. Finally, the knock came. Loung, her brother and sister were sitting on the steps of their shack as the sunset flamed red and gold, when two Khmer soldiers appeared and asked for their father. Ung watched her adored father until he was out of sight, knowing she would never see him again.

The Trauma Continues

Many years later in the US, she realised that her stomach would contort every time she saw a red-gold sunset. "When trauma occurs, it doesn't display itself with an explanation, it doesn't come with a guide book about why you get it—this is why your stomach hurts when you see a sunset. I could have enjoyed many more sunsets if I had realised it sooner!"

A few months later, Ung's mother sent away her three children, Kim, Chou and Loung, explaining that they would be safer as orphans. At a child labour camp, Loung—then aged eight—was selected to train as a soldier. One day she was overcome by a longing to see her mother, but by the time she reached the village, her mother and baby sister had gone, taken by soldiers to join the ranks of Cambodia's "disappeared".

"People would tell Ung she was 'the lucky one', but it wasn't as easy as that."

As Pol Pot's regime crumbled, the five remaining Ung siblings were reunited. Loung's eldest brother Meng was determined to leave Cambodia and paid a smuggler to take him and his wife to Thailand, from where they could leave for the West.

He had enough money for one other person, and chose Loung because he thought she, as the youngest, would adapt most easily to a new way of life. She still wonders what would have happened if he had chosen one of the others. Her second book traces the parallel stories of her own life in Vermont and her sister's life in a jungle village with no electricity or running water, the country around strewn with land mines. Undergoing an arranged marriage at 18, Chou quickly became the mother of five children and is a grandmother at 38.

People would tell Ung she was "the lucky one", but it wasn't as easy as that. "I went through being a child soldier, losing

The Day Pa Disappeared

Pa walks away with a soldier on either side of him. I stand there and wave to him. I watch Pa's figure get smaller and smaller, and still I wave to him, hoping he will turn around and wave back. He never does. I watch until his figure disappears into the horizon of red and gold. When I can no longer see Pa, I turn around and go inside our house, where Ma sits in the corner of the room crying. I have seen Pa leave the house many times in Phnom Penh, but I have never seen her this upset. In my heart I know the truth, but my mind cannot accept the reality of what this all means.

Loung Ung, First They Killed My Father:
A Daughter of Cambodia Remembers.
New York: HarperCollins, 2000.

my parents, living in a refugee camp, then I flew 6,000 miles and that was supposed to be it. Why wasn't I better already? Why wasn't my English perfect? Why didn't I know the American way? It's not over for me, it's not over for my sister, it still goes on."

When a low-flying plane passed, or a firework went off, she flinched. While her classmates were worrying about getting a date for the prom, she was having nightmares about being raped by Khmer Rouge soldiers. She felt a sadness inside that she could not express.

Self-Censorship

At home, her brother and sister-in-law had an unspoken agreement not to talk about the past. Such is the refugee's dilemma: suppressing memories in order to blend in, make a new life. "It was self-censorship of the worst kind," Ung says. "But in America, everything about us was different, our skin, our speech, our way of life, our craving for rice three times a day. When we went to buy a 75lb bag of rice, people would ask us if we owned a store!

"We wanted to be like everybody else, model citizens. There were many things we couldn't change, our skin colour, our slanted eyes, our speech patterns, but the story we didn't have to tell. We didn't change it, we just ignored it."

One night when Ung was 16, she took an overdose of painkillers, but hearing her nieces crying in the next room she vomited up the pills. That same night, she picked up a pen and began to write the story which would later be published as *First They Killed My Father*. "It was my therapy. There's something about writing, channelling your thoughts into your fingers, into a pen, into the page, that was very powerful. When I was writing I had a voice, the voice I had I believed no one wanted to hear." She has been back to Cambodia frequently since she was reunited with Chou in 1995, slewing off her American life to sleep in a hammock, wash in a river, eat fried crickets. "It helps that I can eat everything they eat, if not more. Growing up in the war, I ate out of garbage cans, I have a stomach of steel!"

"'I think the journey to healing is very individual, very unique. There's no real final destination, there's no real closure.'"

The Journey Toward Healing

But she knows her wounds have not fully healed. "I think the journey to healing is very individual, very unique. There's no real final destination, there's no real closure. You do the best you can, bits and pieces. This year, I might only be working on my sister, next year I might decide to work on my brother."

After a period as an activist fronting a campaign against land mines, she is now taking a back seat. Important as the work is, she has also come to value the rhythm of an ordinary life. Living in Cleveland, Ohio, where she is married to Mark, a property developer, she is taking some time out and plans to write a novel: "It's funny, it's irrelevant, probably no one will ever publish it, but it's fun."

"It dawned on me that I wanted to have a good time," she says, slightly shamefaced. "It's a bit selfish, I'm going through guilt about it. But with the second book, I realised how much I enjoyed writing. I've been spending a lot of time reading books which are not about death, murder or genocide. It's pure joy.

"I'm so blessed. I know most people have to wait until their retirement to do this. I am having the most wonderful time." Perhaps, in a small way, the lucky child feels lucky after all.

Former Ugandan Child Soldier Helps Others Experience Childhood

Edd McCracken

In the following viewpoint, Edd McCracken shares the story of China Keitetsi, a former child soldier from Uganda. When she was just nine years old, Keitetsi ran away from her abusive parents and joined the National Resistance Army (NRA), because they gave her a place to sleep. At first Keitetsi was scared by all the violence in the NRA, but eventually she learned to view violence and her gun as her way of life. After she escaped the NRA, she eventually made her way to Denmark, where she became a campaigner for child soldiers. McCracken is a journalist for the Sunday Herald.

As you read, consider the following questions:

1. What kinds of things did Keitetsi talk about with the other children in the NRA?

2. How were the children in the NRA paid?

3. What are some of the ways Keitetsi has helped other child soldiers?

Edd McCracken, "My Life as a Soldier: At the Age of Nine a Rifle Was Her Best Friend. By the Time She Was 12, She Had Killed Many Times. When She Was 18, She Was Forced to Flee Her Home Country, Fearing for Her Life. Now, Living and Writing in Denmark, China Keitetsi Talks to Edd Mccracken About Her Experiences as a Child Soldier and How She Is Helping Other Children Trapped by War," *Sunday Herald* (Glasgow, Scotland), September 12, 2004, p. 12. Copyright © 2004 Herald & Times Group. Reproduced by permission.

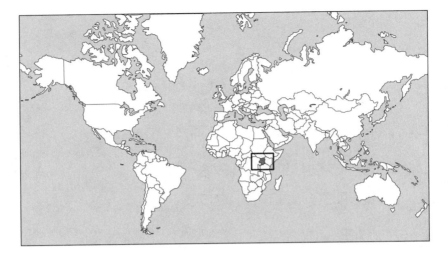

"Of course all these things I have seen, lived in and survived, have left me feeling very, very old. But at the same time I feel like a six-year-old kid too."

China Keitetsi

China Keitetsi never had a childhood. When she should have been playing with her friends, dating boys, and studying at school, she was taking part in a bloody war in the African nation of Uganda. China was a child soldier. Like thousands of child soldiers around the world, she had no time to be young. There were no holidays, no family get-togethers, no part-time jobs, nothing that you associate with growing up. The army stole China Keitetsi's childhood. "It was taken away forever," says the 27-year-old. "You are not allowed to be a kid. All you hear is 'Soldier, come here'. Nobody says 'child, come, I'll protect you.'"

China's parents split up when she was only several months old. Her father remarried, but both he and her stepmother beat China and her sisters. So China fled home and fell into the arms of the National Resistance Army (NRA). It was 1986. She was just nine years old. "They took me in, showed me a place to sleep, then I had to be a part of them," she explains.

"And of course, the first moments when I saw the kids, going 'left-right', it was so nice the way they were swinging their arms and beating their feet to the ground."

Learning to Hate the Enemy

Entranced by the NRA, she soon found herself training with many other child soldiers, fighting for Yoweri Museveni's army and attempting to overthrow President Milton Obote. They were all given guns. Soon after joining, she saw her first taste of the brutal civil war and, naturally for a nine-year-old, it terrified her. "At first I was scared, what with seeing the dead soldiers of the government, the enemy, and seeing people looting from the dead people."

But, China and her fellow child soldiers could not remain spectators for long. "We used to tie their arms behind their back, beating them down on their knees," she says with a slow, sadness in her voice. "Later you had to not let that affect you because when you looked around, all the kids were behaving in the same way. They seemed happy to torture."

"The life of a child soldier is a million miles away from what we consider normal."

And did she kill people? She sighs, long and heavy, before she answers: "Yes."

She explains why she killed with the brutal clarity of a child. "They gave us a gun and the gun was to kill. The gun was for the enemy. The gun was meant for the enemy. Inside of us it was like, if it is the enemy he has no right to live. That means he's already dead. He is nothing. We had to hate the person that our boss hated."

The Gun Was Her Identity

The life of a child soldier is a million miles away from what we consider normal. While most teenagers in Scotland will be discussing what they did at the weekend, when you are 12 years old and fighting in a bloody war, who the best football team is seems irrelevant. "We talked about different things, about what is the best gun, which gun doesn't jam. But we never talked about our feelings," says China. "The only thing most of us were doing was to impress each other. It was like a game: Who's the coolest? Who's the commander? Who's best at beating the captured prisoner or suspect?"

The child soldiers in the NRA were paid only in cigarettes, so China became a chain smoker from the age of nine. As well as their measly pay, the discipline given out to the children in the NRA was terrifyingly harsh. If they were caught stealing food, for example, they were shot. China had to be part of the firing squads that killed many of her friends. The child soldiers lived in constant fear. China's boss abused and beat her, a common experience for most female child soldiers. She wanted to use the gun the NRA gave her against him, but fear stopped her trigger finger. A lot of her friends were not so lucky. "If you killed your boss you had to commit suicide which many did because they knew they would face firing squad. They had the choice of living with the pain, killing the boss and being killed, or kill the boss and kill yourself," she recalls. So when in 1995, China refused the advances of an officer and was then accused of stealing weapons, she knew what she had to do: leave or be shot. She left not just the army, but her son, Moses, whom she gave birth to when she was just 14. She admits she left "at a heavy price". Following a bus ride through Kenya, Tanzania, Zambia, and Zimbabwe, she arrived in South Africa. Without being able to carry her gun, China felt vulnerable. "It was like my identity was suddenly lost," she says. "When I was sleeping I had to put a pillow on my chest because we were told that the gun was our mother, was our friend. So I think that in my life the person I have ever felt closest to, and the person who gave me strength and power, was the gun."

Listening to the Voices of Child Soldiers

The painful stories of the child soldiers of Uganda will break your heart wide open if you allow them access to the deep places within your spirit. All the unseen and unknown children of our time who bear crushing burdens can be encountered in their eyes alone. If you listen with your heart to their voices you will be unable to turn away. All of humanity is propelled forward when we make a choice to be in solidarity with extremely vulnerable youth and help end the plight of children in armed conflict.

Donald H. Dunson,
Child, Victim, Soldier: The Loss of Innocence in Uganda.
New York: Orbis Books, 2008.

Fighting Now to Provide Hope

Her time in South Africa was incredibly fraught. She suffered post-traumatic stress, gave birth to a daughter but had to give her up as she drifted from job to job, before being kidnapped by the Uganda secret police and held for six months. She managed to escape, and in 1999 the UN High Commissioner for Refugees sent China to Denmark, where she lives today. It is a place where she no longer craves for her gun. "Since I came to Denmark three years ago, I have stopped missing the gun. I feel protected. In Denmark it is even against the law to have even a small knife with you. So I feel there is no need for a gun and nothing to protect myself against."

Now China fights only to give hope to child soldiers. She is an active campaigner, raising their plight around the world. She has addressed the general assembly of the United Nations, spoken on behalf of human rights group Amnesty International, and rubbed shoulders with celebrities like Harrison Ford and Robert De Niro while pleading her cause. China has also built a home for ex-child soldiers in the civil war-ravaged country of Rwanda. "I talk about this as much as I can, hoping the other kids would be saved," she explains. "I think I have done a good job. Since my book and since I began to strongly talk about this, I feel there is a little difference. I feel certain countries are frightened to use child soldiers, but before they could use children and no one would say anything."

"'I wish [Scottish teenagers] feel lucky and appreciate all they have got—their presents, their parents, everything.'"

And last month, after a 10-year separation, she was reunited with her son, Moses. There were no tears at the reunion because "I've learned to hide my feelings, they are deep inside". But Moses is now living with China in Denmark so she is learning to be a mother for the first time.

Before we finish our conversation she stops me. She has a message for Scottish teenagers: "I wish they feel lucky and appreciate all they have got—their presents, their parents, everything. Many children will die without ever having that feeling of having a parent, a home in your country, to be loved. I really hope they [Scottish teenagers] feel like the luckiest people."

Former Child Soldier from Democratic Republic of the Congo Now Works as a Carpenter

Bent Jorgen Perlmutt

In the following viewpoint, Bent Jorgen Perlmutt tells the story of former child soldier Maisha, who joined the Mayi-Mayi militia when he was fifteen. After serving as a spy for a year and seeing his friends killed and his village burned, Maisha escaped and joined a UNICEF-sponsored organization for the reintegration of child soldiers into civilian society. Maisha eventually took on an apprenticeship as a carpenter and then was given an internship with the top carpentry firm in Goma. Not all former child soldiers have been as fortunate as Maisha, and although many are now being reintegrated into civilian life, many others are being recruited by the Mayi-Mayi and their opponents. Perlmutt is a contributor to UNICEF and an internationally-lauded documentarian and narrative filmmaker, having produced, among others, three short films on child soldiers in the Congo.

As you read, consider the following questions:

1. What is the RCD?

2. According to Jason Stearns, what percentage of the militia forces is made up of children?

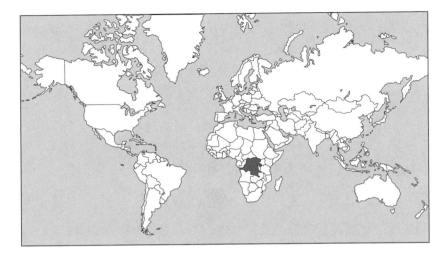

3. Who is Graça Machel?

A decade after the United Nations issued a landmark report on children affected by armed conflict, the context of conflict has changed dramatically. A strategic review of the Graça Machel report is now under way to address this issue for the next 10 years. Here is one of a series of stories testifying to the importance of that review, 'Machel plus 10', scheduled for launch on 17 October.

Goma, Democratic Republic of the Congo, 16 October 2007—Maisha (not his real name) was 15 when he joined the Mayi-Mayi militia, a loose coalition of Congolese soldiers that emerged a decade ago in opposition to the Rwandan-backed Rassemblement Congolais pour la Démocratie (RCD).

According to Jason Stearns, a Nairobi-based senior analyst in the International Crisis Group, children make up 40 to 50 percent of the militia forces.

The Mayi-Mayi recruit children through force or manipulation. They also play on superstition to increase their ranks. 'Mayi' is a Swahili word for water, and the Mayi-Mayi say that magic powers turn bullets directed at them to water. They tell children that they, too, will become indestructible and can protect their families and communities from invaders.

Fleeing from Violence. Maisha joined for all these reasons. He liked to quote the Mayi-Mayi motto: 'Tunafia nchi yetu' (We die for our country).

As one of the brightest students in his class, Maisha was a good candidate for intelligence work. He was a Mayi-Mayi spy for over a year, but after seeing many of his friends killed and his own village burned, he decided to flee. He subsequently enrolled in the Centre pour Transit et Orientation (CTO), a UNICEF-sponsored reintegration centre for children associated with armed groups.

After six months among former combatants at CTO, Maisha began an apprenticeship in which he learned carpentry, mechanics and masonry. Today he has an internship at the top carpentry firm in Goma.

"'Mayi' is a Swahili word for water, and the Mayi-Mayi say that magic powers turn bullets directed at them to water."

Uncertain Futures for Many. Not all former combatants are able to right their lives as successfully as Maisha has done, however. Many child soldiers face a more difficult reintegration into society, because of either a lack of education or traumatic psychological damage.

In eastern Congo alone, there are an estimated 30,000 children associated with armed groups. As Maisha did, most of them fill non-combatant positions such as spies, porters, cooks, domestic servants and sexual slaves.

Although many have now gone through a reintegration process, hundreds are still being recruited every day by both the Mayi-Mayi and the RCD.

'Machel plus 10'. Evaluating the needs of child combatants is part of an ongoing review of the landmark study on children and armed conflict issued more than a decade ago by the

United Nations. Authored by Graça Machel in 1996, the report identified demobilization and reintegration programmes for children as important actions for the international community to take.

"Many child soldiers face a more difficult reintegration into society, because of either a lack of education or traumatic psychological damage."

The context of conflict has changed dramatically in the decade since the Machel report. While there has been significant progress in addressing the issue of child recruitment, unacceptable numbers of boys and girls continue to serve as porters, cooks, messengers and fighters, as well as for sexual purposes, in armed conflicts in at least 18 countries.

To further protect the rights of children in conflict over the next decade, the 'Machel plus 10' review, scheduled to be launched at events in New York tomorrow, recommends:

- Universal adherence to international norms

- Ending impunity for violations against children

- Promoting justice for children

- And supporting inclusive strategies for the reintegration of children associated with armed groups.

VIEWPOINT

Former Child Soldier from Sierra Leone Is Now Author and Child Rights Advocate

Naveed Malik, interviewing Ishmael Beah

Sierra Leone is one of many countries in the world that exploits children by handing them guns and asking them to participate in war. Ishmael Beah was one of these children, until his escape in 1997. Today, Beah is a rap musician, a best-selling author, and a child rights advocate. In this interview, he speaks about his music, his writing, and the importance of advocacy. Naveed Malik became co–editor in chief of the Kennedy School Review *in 2006.*

As you read, consider the following questions:

1. What trade fueled the war in Sierra Leone?

2. What opportunity does Ishmael Beah cite as being unavailable to him in Sierra Leone?

3. What is the purpose of the document known as *The Paris Principles*?

T he best-selling author of *A Long Way Gone: Memoirs of a Boy Soldier*, Ishmael Beah now lives in New York and works for Human Rights Watch. On 14 March 2007, Beah vis-

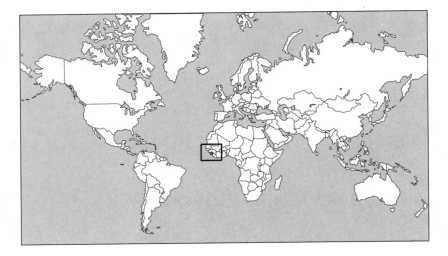

ited the John F. Kennedy School of Government at Harvard University to take part in a JFK Jr. Forum event entitled, "I Was a Child Soldier."

Naveed Malik had the pleasure of interviewing Beah at that time. We are grateful to Andrea Rossi, a visiting fellow from UNICEF [United Nations Children's Fund], who arranged for the personal meeting.

Kennedy School Review [KSR]

Ishmael, in reading your book, I was struck by the number of instances in which your cassettes of American music got you out of trouble. Do you still listen to hip hop today?

Beah

Yes, I still do love and listen to hip hop.

KSR

Who are your favorite artists?

Beah

Mostly old school and underground hip hop, but there are some emcees that I still regard highly; Common, Mos Def, Talib Kweli, and Outkast are a few.

What Is Home

KSR

Can you tell us about your first trip back to Sierra Leone?
Beah

I went back to Sierra Leone—home—in June of 2006. I left in 1997 and this was my first trip back. I traveled with people from VH1 and Article 19 films who were making a documentary called *Bling: A Planet Rock* that aimed at educating American rappers about the war, the blood diamond trade that fueled the war, and generally introducing them to the people and culture of Sierra Leone. We took with us three musicians: Raekwon from the Wu-Tang Clan, Tego Calderón, and Paul Wall. My role was to bridge the two cultures since I have lived in both and have a strong interest in hip-hop music. We visited Freetown, the capital, and went to Kono, the diamond area.

KSR

Did you learn the whereabouts of any of your friends mentioned in the book?
Beah

A lot of them didn't survive the war, but some did and I have been able to reconnect with them. Some live abroad and others still back home in Sierra Leone, where I was able to find them during my visit.

"I still carry memories from that war that bring me flashbacks and nightmares."

KSR

Do you still have flashbacks from the war?
Beah

I still carry memories from that war that bring me flashbacks and nightmares. But I have learned to live with them, to fully understand and transform them so that they no longer disturb me as they used to. I have come to use my memories and experiences from that war as instructional tools that guide me to live in peace and appreciate my second life, as I like to think of it.

KSR

In your second life, where is home?

Beah

I intend to live in both America and Sierra Leone. Regardless of what happened in Sierra Leone, it is my home; it is where I received the early traditional and cultural upbringing that shaped my identity and taught me a deep understanding of life that gave me the strength to be able to heal from that war. As much as I love Sierra Leone, however, there are certain opportunities that I can't get there. For example, I can't currently be a writer in Sierra Leone. So for this reason I stay in the United States. However, I will do whatever I can to contribute to the future of my nation.

Current Endeavors

KSR

To that end, can you tell us about the Ishmael Beah Foundation?

Beah

The Ishmael Beah Foundation, which is now incorporated and should have a Web site up and running soon, will provide educational and vocational opportunities for children whose lives have been affected by war during and after the rehabilitation process so as to prevent them from reentering a life of violence. The foundation will provide financial support for local organizations that are already doing this work and will create programs to do follow-up work after children leave the rehabilitation centers. The foundation's initial work will start in Sierra Leone, and we will then expand to other nations.

KSR

I take it you want to write more. What ideas do you have for the next book?

Everybody Gets Used to It

We must have been walking for days, I do not really remember, when suddenly two men put us at gunpoint and motioned, with their guns, for us to come closer. We walked in between two rows of men carrying machine guns, AK-47s, G3s, and RPGs. Their faces were dark, as if they had bathed them in charcoal, and they stared intensely at us with their extremely red eyes. When we got to the back of the line, there were four men lying on the ground, their uniforms soaked with blood. One of them lay on his stomach, and his eyes were wide open and still; his insides were spilling onto the ground. I turned away, and my eyes caught the smashed head of another man. Something inside his brain was still pulsating and he was breathing. I felt nauseated. Everything began to spin around me. One of the soldiers was looking at me, chewing something and smiling. He took a drink from his water bottle and threw the remaining water at my face.

"You will get used to it, everybody does eventually," he said.

Ishmael Beah,
A Long Way Gone: Memoirs of a Boy Soldier.
New York: Farrar, Straus and Giroux, 2007.

Beah

I already have a few chapters of my first novel, but it is still too early to discuss it in much detail. I have also received another interesting request a lot after readings: People want to know how I got here as my current book ends when I am still in Africa. So there is a tremendous interest in a sequel. I am not sure which will come first, the novel or the sequel.

Advocacy Is Essential

KSR

You've already accomplished a great deal through the book and your advocacy work. What about people who don't have your incredible personal story and might not be able to reach and affect people as you do? What is the best course of action we can take to advance this issue?

Beah

Firstly, I hope that this book will compel individuals to want to find out more about the issue because, through this, they will be able to find organizations that they can support to prevent this issue, places they can volunteer to work, and a whole host of other options. Second, I believe that advocacy is very important as it serves as a constant reminder for people to pay attention to a continuing problem. Advocacy will also push individuals to empower themselves with more information about the issue, so that they will be in a position to pressure their governments to work toward the prevention of the use of children in war—governments that are both affected and not affected.

"Much has been done and much more remains to be done."

KSR

The number of children currently in armed conflict is estimated between three hundred thousand and half a million. In which parts of the world is the problem of child soldiers the worst today?

Beah

There are so many, but a few countries are Uganda, the Democratic Republic of the Congo, Colombia, Sri Lanka, Nepal, Myanmar, and so on. It is a worldwide problem, not just an African problem, as it is widely perceived.

KSR

What relationship should advocates have with politicians and policy makers? And what in your view must the latter do to address child soldiering?

Beah

It is absolutely critical [for advocates] to work with governments to prevent the use of children in war, and much has been done to make this happen. This cooperation requires careful negotiation and compromise, and I just hope that there will be continuous and rigorous support from governments, and more political will to strengthen the work of UN [United Nations] agencies and NGOs [nongovernmental organizations]. It is absolutely essential to have this cooperation so as to effectively heal those children affected by war in all capacities and to further prevent the occurrences of these wars. Much has been done and much more remains to be done. And I advocate for preventive measures, things that get rid of the practices that give rise to war in the first place.

KSR

If, during a war, an aid worker has intermittent access to active child soldiers, what do you feel they must do to maximize the child's welfare? Can they effectively begin the healing process at this stage, even though those children will return to fighting after their meeting?

Beah

The methods vary from situation to situation even though there are some commonalities. But one point that I will make is that the aid workers have to carefully negotiate with warlords in order to be able to get them to release children. There is a document known as *The Paris Principles* and [*The Paris*] *Commitments* that UNICEF [United Nations Children's Fund] and other NGOs have put together to examine the practical measures that can be used to effectively help children affected by war. This *Paris Principles* came from a careful study of practices that have worked and those that have failed, and how these can be improved to make rehabilitation and the re-integration process effective in the best interests of the child. I would recommend that you take a look at it. It should be available online.

KSR

You were removed from conflict and rehabilitated through the efforts of UNICEF and its partner organizations. From your firsthand experience, most of which is described in the book, what recommendations can you offer groups carrying out this work to improve their effectiveness?

Beah

A thorough understanding of the culture and sensitivity to the traditions of the people they are trying to help. Also, this kind of work requires perseverance and tremendous patience.

Future Endeavors

KSR

During your visit to the Kennedy School, you expressed an interest in pursuing graduate studies. Do you have a particular focus in mind?

Beah

I am interested in pursing a dual degree, a M.A. in international affairs and a J.D. in international law.

KSR

Ishmael, you're a best-selling author, a famous child rights advocate, and currently work at the most prestigious human rights organization in America. What more do you hope to accomplish by going to graduate school?

Beah

I want my involvement with preventing the use of children in war, and in generally promoting the respect for the human rights of all people, to go beyond just advocacy. Through this graduate program, or any other higher degree, I will be able to participate in high-level policy work, thereby bringing firsthand experience to make policies that work.

Periodical Bibliography

AllAfrica   "Burundi's Former Child Soldiers Strive to Re-Enter Society," August 5, 2009. www.allafrica.com.

BBC News   "Nepal Child Soldiers Being Freed," July 17, 2009. http://news.bbc.co.uk.

Bruce Bower   "Lost Are Found: Child Soldiers Can Reenter, Thrive in Former Community," *Science News*, June 7, 2008.

Christine Dell'Amore   "A Soldier's Story: After More than a Decade of Warfare, Joseph Duo Is Finding That Peace Takes Some Getting Used To," *Smithsonian*, February 2006.

Daphne Eviatar   "U.S. Will Transfer Gitmo Child Soldier to Civilian Court, but Still Won't Let Him Go," *Washington Independent*, July 27, 2009. http://washingtonindependent.com.

IRIN News   "NEPAL: Agencies Urge Rehabilitation for Former Child Soldiers," July 26, 2009.

Know Your World Extra   "A New Life: A Former Child Soldier in Africa Raps About His Past," January 25, 2008.

Angus McKenzie   "A Fireman in Sudan: A Bit of Can-do and He's Building a School with Child Soldiers, *Presbyterian Record*, March 2007.

Mary Riddell   "Rebuilding the Lives of Congo's Child Soldiers," *Telegraph*, July 16, 2009. www.telegraph.co.uk.

For Further Discussion

Chapter 1

1. In Viewpoint 1-3, Jeffrey Gettleman states that although "Africa didn't invent the modern underage soldier," child soldiers of today's Africa have a unique character. How does Gettleman describe this character? How does Namrita Talwar's viewpoint (1-2) support Gettleman's statement? Do you think Mirjana Rakela (Viewpoint 1-1) and Charles Geisler and Niousha Roshani (Viewpoint 1-4) would agree that non-African nations' use of child soldiers is equally brutal? Do you agree with Gettleman? Why or why not?

Chapter 2

1. According to P.W. Singer in Viewpoint 2-1, "Poorer children are typically more vulnerable to being pulled into conflict and are overrepresented in child soldier groups." Would the authors of the other viewpoints in this chapter agree with Singer? Why or why not? Do you agree that adolescents suffering from poverty are more vulnerable to negative situations than others? Why or why not?

Chapter 3

1. This chapter contains viewpoints that view international efforts to help child soldiers in a positive way and viewpoints that say not nearly enough is being done to help the situation. Which authors think more must be done? Of these, what is the author's background or personal experience with child soldiers? Do you think a person's background would affect whether her or she views the efforts in a positive way? Why or why not? Do you believe

enough is being done to help the child soldier situation? Would your perspective change if you lived in an area directly impacted by child soldiering?

Chapter 4

1. Viewpoints in this chapter focus on the lives of former child soldiers. While each of these individuals copes with the brutal past in his or her own way (writing, music, advocating for children's rights, etc.), none are able to completely move beyond the past. As former Sierra Leone child soldier Ishmael Beah states in Viewpoint 4-4, when asked about where he considers home, "I intend to live in both America and Sierra Leone. Regardless of what happened in Sierra Leone, it is my home." How do the other subjects of the viewpoints in this chapter hold on to their pasts, while still moving forward? Do you think it is common for victims of violence to hold on to their painful pasts? Do you think doing so is an essential part of the healing process? Why or why not?

Organizations to Contact

The editors have compiled the following list of organizations concerned with the issues debated in this book. The descriptions are derived from materials provided by the organizations. All have publications or information available for interested readers. The list was compiled on the date of publication of the present volume; the information provided here may change. Be aware that many organizations take several weeks or longer to respond to inquiries, so allow as much time as possible.

Amnesty International (AI)

1 Easton Street, London WC1X 0DW
  United Kingdom
+44-2074135500 • fax: +44-2079561157
e-mail: www.amnesty.org/en/contact
Web site: www.amnesty.org

Amnesty International (AI) is a worldwide organization that campaigns for human rights for all individuals. As part of this goal, Amnesty International campaigns against the use of child soldiers. The organization's Web site provides details about its campaigns to stop the abuse of individuals around the globe including child soldiers.

Child Soldier Relief (CSR)

Web site: http://childsoldierrelief.com

Child Soldier Relief's (CSR's) mission is to provide current and historical information about child soldiers to best advocate on behalf of child soldiers. CSR research informs the public of issues relating to child soldiers through films, books, documentaries, television shows, and online sources available on its Web site. CSR compiles information such as a current list of countries using child soldiers and updates on current wars that involve child soldiers.

Coalition to Stop the Use of Child Soldiers

9 Marshalsea Road, 4th Floor, London   SE1 1EP
   United Kingdom
+44-(0)2073674110 • fax: +44-(0)2073674129
e-mail: info@child-soldiers.org
Web site: www.child-soldiers.org

Coalition to Stop the Use of Child Soldiers works to prevent the recruitment and use of child soldiers, to demobilize them, and to help them rehabilitate and reintegrate into society. To achieve this, the coalition produces the *Child Soldiers Global Report* every three years, which spreads awareness about child soldiers across the globe. The report is available on the organization's Web site.

Defence for Children International (DCI)

Rue de Varembé 1, Case Postale 88, Geneva 20   CH-1211
   Switzerland
+41-227340558 • fax: +41-227401145
e-mail: info@dci-is.org
Web site: www.defenceforchildren.org

Defence for Children International (DCI) is an independent organization dedicated to protecting and promoting children's rights on the global, regional, national, and local levels. DCI, which is represented in forty countries worldwide and was founded in 1979, was a major force behind the adoption of the United Nations Convention on the Rights of the Child. DCI's Web site provides information about juvenile justice and other rights, and links regarding children's rights worldwide.

Free the Children

233 Carlton Street, Toronto, Ontario   M5A 2L2
   Canada
(416) 925-5894 • fax: (416) 925-8242
e-mail: youth@freethechildren.com
Web site: www.freethechildren.com

Free the Children, in partnership with the United Nations Office of the Special Representative for Children and Armed Conflict, launched the Youth Ambassadors for Peace Project. The project's mission is to use education and action campaigns to mobilize the youth of the world to build a children-to-children network to help end the use of child soldiers. The two main vehicles toward this goal are the "War Is Not a Game Campaign" and the "Schools for Peace Initiative," which are both detailed on Free the Children's Web site.

Human Rights Watch (HRW)

350 Fifth Avenue, 34th Floor, New York, NY   10118-3299
(212) 290-4700 • fax: (212) 736-1300
e-mail: hrwnyc@hrw.org
Web site: www.hrw.org

Human Rights Watch (HRW) is among the world's leading organizations committed to defending and protecting human rights. It works to make legal and moral changes to bring justice to people worldwide. Its Web site publishes articles and provides resources about child soldiers and human rights issues around the world.

International Action Network on Small Arms (IANSA)

Development House, 56-64 Leonard Street
London   EC2A 4LT
  United Kingdom
+44-2070650870 • fax: +44-2070650871
e-mail: contact@iansa.org
Web site: www.iansa.org

International Action Network on Small Arms (IANSA) is a network of eight hundred organizations representing a global movement to stop gun violence. IANSA works to make the world safer from gun violence by lobbying for stronger gun regulations and improved controls on arms exports. IANSA's key issues are listed on its Web site; among these is reducing the number of weapons that land in the arms of child soldiers. The Web site also includes an extensive list of nongovernmental organizations (NGOs) that campaign on the issue of child soldiers and publications about child soldiers.

Invisible Children Inc.

1620 Fifth Avenue, Suite 400, San Diego, CA   92101
(619) 562-2799 • fax: (619) 660-0576
e-mail: info@invisiblechildren.com
Web site: www.invisiblechildren.com

Invisible Children Inc.'s purpose is to use the power of stories to change lives around the world. In particular, the organization is dedicated to ending the use of child soldiers in Uganda. Its first film, *Invisible Children: Discover the Unseen*, portrays Uganda's child soldier situation and calls upon viewers to help out. The film sparked a movement that has reached millions of students around the globe.

Save the Children UK

1 St. John's Lane, London   EC1M 4AR
  United Kingdom
+44-(0)2070126400
e-mail: supporter.care@savethechildren.org.uk
Web site: www.savethechildren.org.uk

Save the Children UK works to ensure children around the world are provided adequate health care, food, education, and protection. To accomplish this, Save the Children provides funds and services to countries in need, and informs the public of crises involving children. Its Web site includes news and information about its active campaigns and a list of resources.

Somali Child Soldier Relief Organization

15 Varna Drive, Toronto, Ontario   M6A 2L6
  Canada
(416) 832-5640
e-mail: somalichildsoldier@yahoo.ca
Web site: www.somalichildsoldier.org

The objective of Somali Child Soldier Relief Organization is to create positive choices for Somali youth, and to discourage them from taking up arms. Somali Child Soldier Relief has teamed up with other organizations to build Mushani, a center for children who might otherwise be lured into becoming child soldiers. Mushani provides youth with shelter, education, food, medicine, and security. More details about its programs are available on Somali Child Soldier Relief Organization's Web site.

United Nations International Children's Emergency Fund (UNICEF)

UNICEF House, 3 United Nations Plaza, New York, NY   10017
(212) 326-7000 • fax: (212) 887-7465
e-mail: www.unicefusa.org/about/contact
Web site: www.unicef.org

United Nations International Children's Emergency Fund (UNICEF) advocates for the rights of children around the globe including ending the use of child soldiers. To realize this goal, UNICEF works with 191 countries and spreads its voice through print, television, radio, podcast, and vodcast, details of which can be found on its Web site. All of UNICEF's publications are focused on improving the lives of children.

War Child International

401 Richmond Street West, Suite 204
Toronto, Ontario   M5V3A8
   Canada
(416) 971-7474 • fax: (416) 971-7946
e-mail: info@warchild.ca
Web site: www.warchild.org

War Child International is a team of organizations that works together to help children affected by war. Its primary goal is to provide hope to children whose lives have been turned upside down by war. War Child International's Web site provides extensive information on child soldiers, the other ways war affects children, and details about what services it provides to children affected by war.

Bibliography of Books

Ishmael Beah	*A Long Way Gone: Memoirs of a Boy Soldier.* New York: Farrar, Straus and Giroux, 2007.
Neil Boothby et al., eds.	*A World Turned Upside Down: Social Ecological Approaches to Children in War Zones.* Bloomfield, CT: Kumarian Press, Inc., 2006.
Jimmie Briggs	*Innocents Lost: When Child Soldiers Go to War.* New York: Basic Books, 2005.
John S. Burnett	*Where Soldiers Fear to Tread: A Relief Worker's Tale of Survival.* New York: Bantam Books, 2005.
Tim Butcher	*Blood River: A Journey to Africa's Broken Heart.* London: Chatto & Windus, 2007.
Donald H. Dunson	*Child, Victim, Soldier: The Loss of Innocence in Uganda.* Maryknoll, NY: Orbis Books, 2008.
Peter Eichstaedt	*First Kill Your Family: Child Soldiers of Uganda and the Lord's Resistance Army.* Chicago: Lawrence Hill Books, 2009.
Scott Gates and Simon Reich, eds.	*Child Soldiers in the Age of Fractured States.* Pittsburgh, PA: University of Pittsburgh Press, 2009.

Alcinda Honwana   *Child Soldiers in Africa.* Philadelphia: University of Pennsylvania Press, 2006.

Human Rights Watch   *My Gun Was as Tall as Me: Child Soldiers in Burma.* New York: Human Rights Watch, 2002.

Emmanuel Jal and Megan Lloyd Davies   *War Child: A Child Soldier's Story.* New York: St. Martin's Press, 2009.

Delia Jarrett-Macauley   *Moses, Citizen & Me.* London: Granta Books, 2005.

Leora Kahn and Luis Moreno-Ocampo   *Child Soldiers.* New York: Power-House Books, 2008.

China Keitetsi   *Child Soldier: Fighting for My Life.* Bellevue, South Africa: Jacana, 2002.

Ahmadou Kourouma   *Allah Is Not Obliged.* New York: Anchor Books, 2007.

Alice LoCicero and Samuel J. Sinclair   *Creating Young Martyrs: Conditions That Make Dying in a Terrorist Attack Seem Like a Good Idea.* Westport, CT: Praeger Security International, 2008.

Charles London   *One Day the Soldiers Came: Voices of Children in War.* New York: Harper-Perennial, 2007.

Faith J.H. McDonnell and Grace Akallo   *Girl Soldier: A Story of Hope for Northern Uganda's Children.* Grand Rapids, MI: Chosen, 2007.

Bryan Mealer

All Things Must Fight to Live: Stories of War and Deliverance in Congo. New York: Bloomsbury, 2008.

Senait Mehari

Heart of Fire: One Girl's Extraordinary Journey from Child Soldier to Soul Singer. London: Profile Books, 2008.

P.W. Singer

Children at War. Berkeley & Los Angeles: University of California Press, 2006.

Loung Ung

First They Killed My Father: A Daughter of Cambodia Remembers. New York: HarperCollins, 2000.

Loung Ung

Lucky Child: A Daughter of Cambodia Reunites with the Sister She Left Behind. New York: HarperCollins, 2005.

Michael Wessells

Child Soldiers: From Violence to Protection. Cambridge, MA: Harvard University Press, 2006.

Index

Geographic headings and page numbers in **boldface** refer to viewpoints about that country or region.

A

Abductions, 30, 55, 64–65, 67–68
Achilles (Greek hero), 15
Acholi people, 30, 35
Acquired Immune Deficiency Syndrome (AIDS), 124, 125–126
Adam, Forbes, 156–158, 160–161
Aden, Qamar, 135
Advocacy efforts, 29, 93, 181–188
Aegeus (Greek king), 15
Afghanistan, child soldiers
  choices of, 70
  Guantánamo Bay, 52
  number of, 24
  prisoner of war status and, 52
  rehabilitation difficulties with, 91
  religion-driven fights by, 36
  suicide missions by, 20, 25, 158
  Taliban and, 51
Africa, 131–135
Africa, child soldiers
  abduction and, 55
  armed movements and, 35–38
  in Ethiopia, 20, 65
  girls as, 56, 135
  initiation ceremonies by, 98–99
  in Kenya, 38, 174
  in Liberia, 41, 67, 72, 160
  location of, 134
  in Namibia, 123–124
  number of, 20, 34

  recruitment of, 131–135
  in Somalia, 35, 133–135, 157
  in South Africa, 38, 145, 148–150, 174–175
  state responsibilities for, 133–135
  See also individual African countries
After They Killed Our Father: A Refugee from the Killing Fields Reunites with the Sister She Left Behind (Ung), 165
AK-47 automatic rifle, 71, 106, 110, 138
al Qaeda (terrorist group), 22, 24–25, 51
Albuquerque, Catarina de, 122
Alley, Patrick, 78
AMBER Alert program, 30
American Revolutionary Army, 87
Amnesty in peace agreements, 133–134
Amnesty International, 16, 175
Angola, child soldiers
  cultural roles *vs.*, 98
  girls as, 56–58, 60
  indigenous healing techniques, 100–102
  reintegration of, 99
Armed movements/groups
  in Africa, 35–38
  challenges with, 158
  impact of, 159
  reduction in, 156–157
  See also Terrorists/terrorism
Army National Guard, 30

Asia, 22, 55, 56, 69, 70, 135
Asthana, Anushka, 74–82

B

Bakayoko, Youssouf, 133
Balkan wars, 25–26
Bamri, Diar, 21–22
Ban Ki-moon, 108
Beah, Ishmael, 37–38, 91, 120–130, 132, 181–188
Becker, Jo, 22–23
Biological and Toxin Weapons Convention, 93
Bishikwabo, Cikuru, 80
Blair, Tony, 76
Boothby, Neil, 37, 147, 148, 150, 153
Bosnia-Croatia conflict, 92
Bowles, Sharon, 26
Boy soldiers
    abuse of, 67–68
    in ancient Greece, 15–17
    number of, 59
    poverty and, 70
    recruitment of, 66–67
    reintegration of, 80, 99–101
Brown, Gordon, 76
Burma, child soldiers, 22–23

C

Cambodia, 164–170
Cambodia, child soldiers
    displacement from home, 165–166
    healing, 164–170, 169–170
    self-censorship, 168–169
    trauma of, 167–168
Camp America, 51
Camp Delta, 49, 51, 52
Camp Justice, 52

Caribbean Community (CARICOM), 124–126
Castro, Fidel, 49
Centre pour Transit et Orientation (CTO), 179
Chemical warfare, 93
Child labor, 15, 44, 94, 115, 140, 167
Child soldiers
    in Cambodia, 164–170
    in Columbia, 39–47, 106–112
    in Democratic Republic of Congo, 74–82, 177–180
    efforts against, 28–31
    global distribution, 19–26
    in Iraq, 113–117
    in Mozambique, 33–38
    number of, 23–25, 34, 59, 85, 132, 179, 186
    in Sierra Leone, 181–188
    treatment after capture, 48–53, 134–135
    in Uganda, 27–32, 171–176
    United States and, 48–53
    See also Boy soldiers; Girl soldiers
Children's Crusade, 47
Christianity, 47
Civil War, 15
Clydedale, Lindsay, 136–141
Coalition to Stop the Use of Child Soldiers, 20, 98, 108, 155–161
Colombia, 39–47, 106–112
Colombia, child soldiers
    abduction and, 67
    abundance of, 39–47
    advocacy for, 186
    displaced children and, 40–41
    girls as, 56, 57
    poverty and, 106–112
    responsibility for, 43–44

societal effects of, 42
solutions for, 46
Colombia's Consultancy on Human Rights and Displacement (CODHES), 40–41, 43
Comic Relief (charity organization), 138–141
Commission for Africa, 76, 81–82
Congolese Rally for Democracy-Goma (RCD-Goma), 65
Convention on the Rights of the Child (CRC)
    Balkan wars and, 25
    capital punishment and, 36
    definition of child by, 14–16
    displaced persons and, 42
    protection of rights, 129
    ratification of, 122
    recruitment ages and, 29, 94, 98
    support of, 26, 123, 125
Coomaraswamy, Radhika, 121
Criminal gangs, 86
Cuba, 49, 51, 53
Curtis, Vincent J., 48–53

D

Dehumanization effects, 88
Democratic Republic of the Congo, 74–82, 177–180
Democratic Republic of the Congo (DRC), child soldiers
    abductions of, 67
    civil war in, 35, 82
    criminal trials in, 134
    displaced children in, 41
    poverty in, 77–78
    rehabilitation of, 74–82, 177–180
    reintegration efforts, 78–81, 104
    resource curse, 78

voluntary recruitment and, 70
war in, 79
Desertion consequences. *See* Escape/desertion
Desocialization effects, 88
Developing Minds Foundation, 108, 111
Development Programme (UN), 40
Disarmament, Demobilisation and Reinsertion (DDR)
    mismanagement of, 160
    rehabilitation and, 93
    reintegration and, 77, 103–104, 158–159
    start of, 79
Displaced children. *See* Internally displaced persons
Domestic violence, 123
Doukaev, Aslan, 23
DousteBlazy, Philippe, 131–132
Drug abuse
    at home, 24
    as soldiers, 26, 35, 84, 86, 110, 138

E

East Asia, 69, 70
El Salvador, child soldiers, 20, 104
Escape/desertion
    death and, 31, 107, 145
    demobilization and, 79
    fostering dependency against, 64
    government retribution for, 36, 157
    from home problems, 28, 55, 76
    from poverty, 106–112
    punishment for, 22, 23, 58
    safety from, 144, 146, 153, 175
Ethiopia, child soldiers, 20, 65

Europe, child soldiers, 25–26, 55, 56, 122

F

Fear tactics, 22–23
First They Killed My Father: A Daughter of Cambodia Remembers (Ung), 165, 168, 169
Flashback triggers, 92
Free Children from War conference, 132
Fuerzas Armadas Revolucionarias de Colombia (FARC), 45–46, 69, 107, 108–112

G

G-8 group, 125
Geisler, Charles, 39–47
Geldof, Bob, 76
General Assembly (UN), 120–130, 133, 175
Geneva Conventions, 36, 52, 85, 93
Genocide, 37, 67–68
Gettleman, Jeffrey, 33–38
Girl soldiers
    abuse of, 55, 56–57, 68
    identity changes in, 59–60
    number of, 20, 59
    psychological impact of, 57–58, 77
    rape and, 31, 56
    reintegration of, 78–79, 103–105, 135, 160
    as wives of rebels, 28, 59
Global Witness campaign group, 78
Grief rituals, 88–89
Gross domestic product (GDP), 28

Guantánamo Bay, Cuba (Gitmo)
    camp design of, 52–53
    child soldiers in, 50
    Khadr, Omar in, 49, 51–52
    legal status of, 51
    U.S. treatment protocol in, 48–53
Guatemala, child soldiers, 22, 67, 90
Guerrilla groups, 42, 90

H

Hackett, Christopher, 124–125
Harnden, Toby, 113–117
Harsch, Ernest, 131–135
Health concerns
    grief rituals, 88–89
    historical comparisons, 86–88
    overview, 84–86
    rehabilitation, 91–94
    in twentieth century, 88–89, 91
    wounds and, 90
    See also Indigenous healing practices
Herbert, Wray, 142–154
Hercules (Greek hero), 15–16
High Commissioner for Refugees (UNHCR), 66, 175
The Holocaust, 92
Homeless children. *See* Internally displaced persons
Houdard, Philippe, 107–108, 111
Human Immunodeficiency Virus (HIV), 124, 125–126
Human Rights Watch
    displaced persons and, 41, 43, 45
    FARC and, 109, 111
    poverty and, 78, 107
    recruitment tactics and, 22–23, 35, 109

Hundred Years' War, 15
Hunger/starvation
    in conflict zones, 69, 73, 93,
      137
    of displace persons, 166
    fear and, 22, 107
    girl soldier vulnerability to,
      124
    military training and, 16, 164
    as recruitment motivation, 77,
      141

I

The Iliad (Homer), 15
Impact of Armed Conflict on Children (Machel), 122
Indigenous healing practices
    adult *vs.* child, 98–99
    reintegration attempts with,
      99–101, 103–105
    symbolism in, 101–103
    theory behind, 97–98
Internal Displacement Monitoring
  Centre (IDMC), 42
Internally displaced persons
  (IDPs)
    in Cambodia, 165–166
    child soldier connection to,
      44–46
    mortality rates of, 42
    number of, 40–41
    recruitment of, 66
    reintegration of, 44, 81
    responsibility for, 43–44
International assistance
    government recruitment and,
      157–158
    by Japan, 128–130
    by Namibia, 123–124
    overview, 120–122, 155–157
    by Portugal, 122–123
    for reintegration, 121–122,
      158–161

    by Sri Lanka, 127–128, 186
    by Sudan, 127, 133
International Children's Emergency Fund (UNICEF)
    advocacy efforts by, 182, 187–188
    education programs by, 16, 126
    Free Children from War conference, 132
    international aid by, 76, 122, 129
    rehabilitation and, 133, 179
    reintegration and, 76–77, 78, 179
International Criminal Court, 29, 94, 134
International Red Cross, 84–85
Invisible Children Inc., 16
Iran, child soldiers, 35–36, 87
Iran–Iraq War, 35–36, 87
Iraq, 113–117
Iraq, child soldiers
    effects of war on, 115, 165
    martyrdom and, 113–117
    as terrorists, 20–22
    in traditional armies, 87
Ishmael Beah Foundation, 184
Israel Defense Forces, 157

J

Japan, 128–130
Jareg, Elizabeth, 60
Joint Task Force 2 (JTF2) commandos, 51

K

Kabila, Laurent-Désiré 69, 82
Kaboy, Pascal, 81
Kalashnikov (rifle), 113
Keitetsi, China, 172–176

Kenya, 38, 174
Khadr, Omar, 49, 51–52, 53
Khmer Rouge, 165–166, 168
Kony, Joseph, 56
Kuebler, William, 51
Kurosaki, Nobuko, 128–129
Kuxukuvala (clinical depression), 152

L

Lancet (journal), 31
Lavally, Francis, 138–139
Laws of War, 84–85, 89
Lebanon, child soldiers, 20
Leopard Brigade (Sirasu Puli), 65
Lhanguene orphanage, 144, 146–147, 150, 151, 153–154
Liberation Tigers of Tamil Eelam (LTTE), 64, 65, 71
Liberia, 41, 67, 72, 160
Life expectancy rates, 14–15
Linares, Beatriz, 108
London Blitz, 92
Long-running conflicts, 34–35
A Long Way Gone: Memoirs of a Boy Soldier (Beah), 37, 91, 181
Lord's Resistance Army (LRA), 27–28, 30, 31, 35, 36, 56, 64
Los Angeles Times (newspaper), 21
Lubanga, Thomas, 64
Lumumba, Patrice, 82

M

Macamo, Alfredo Betuel, 143–144, 150, 151, 153, 154
Machel, Graça 121, 122, 133, 178–180
Macouvele, Angelo Jose, 148
Magic as manipulation, 37–38
Malik, Naveed, 181–188

Manipulation tactics, 20–21, 37–38
Mansfield, Susan, 164–170
Martyrdom, 113–117
Marxist government, 38, 145
Massingue, Israel Armando, 148–149, 150, 151, 154
Mathenge, Penninah, 77, 79
Mauer, Maggie, 108
Mayi-Mayi militia, 178–179
Mbuende, Kaire Munionganda, 123
McCracken, Edd, 171–176
McFarland, Maria, 109, 111
McKay, Susan, 54–60
Middle East, 20, 55, 121
Military Commissions Act, 51
Military schools for children, 126
Millennium Development Goals (MDGs), 124, 125, 127–128
Mobutu, Joseph, 82
Mohamed, Abdelhamid Abidin, 127
Mondlane, Rosalina, 151–152, 154
Morals/morality, 47, 57, 68, 86, 92, 133
Mortality rates, 42, 125, 128, 141
Movement for Assistance and Promotion of Rural Communities (MAPCO), 138, 140
Mozambique, 33–38, 142–154
Mozambique, child soldiers
    adult initiation practices, 99
    exploitation of, 33–38
    girls as, 56
    healing mechanisms for, 142–154
    health problems with, 90
    history of, 144–146
    indigenous healing practices for, 103

long-running conflicts and, 34–35

long-term impact on, 143–144

loss of earning potential by, 148–150

magic as manipulation, 37–38

measures of success, 150–151

safe havens for, 146–147

Mozambique National Resistance. *See* Renamo

Mudaqiq, Mohammad Amin, 24–25

Murphy, Helen, 106–112

Museveni, Yoweri, 173

Muslims, 25, 47

N

Namibia, 123–124

Napoleonic Wars (1803–1815), 15

National Resistance Army (NRA), 172–173, 174

Nazi Party, 35

Ngevao, Gaspard, 141

Nongovernmental organizations (NGOs), 20, 40, 41, 93, 132, 187

Nortey, Dedo, 80

North Atlantic Treaty Organization (NATO), 25

O

Obote, Milton, 173

Official development assistance (ODA), 125

Optional Protocols, 29, 122

P

Pakistan, child soldiers, 25, 158

Palestine, child soldiers, 20, 36, 71, 127, 157

Paramilitary groups, 42

Parental complicity, 70–71

Paris Commitments document, 132–133, 135, 187

Peace process, 29–30, 47, 133–134

Pearn, J., 83–95

Perlmutt, Bent Jorgen, 177–180

Peru, 55, 67

Philippines, child soldiers, 56

Pinheiro, Paulo, 129

Plato (Greek philosopher), 16

Pol Pot, 164–167

Portugal, 122–123, 144–145

Post-traumatic stress disorder (PTSD), 88, 89, 151, 152

Poverty

child soldiers and, 21–22, 69–70, 77–78

children's rights and, 123

in Columbia, 106–112

death *vs.*, 109–112

Psychological impact, 57–58, 77, 89, 153–154

Q

Quive, Joaquim Fernando, 143–144, 151–154

R

Radio Free Europe/Radio Liberty, 21

Rakela, Mirjana, 19–26

Rape concerns

by child solider recruiters, 68, 76, 86, 164, 168

rampages, 67

reintegration and, 78–81, 104, 135, 138, 160

in Uganda, 31, 56

as violation of sacredness, 104

Rebel wives, 28, 59

Recruitment tactics
abduction, 64–65, 67–68
in Africa, 131–135
for child soldiers, 22, 23–25
choices against, 70–71
genocide and, 67–68
by governments, 157–158
process of, 65–66, 178
protection against, 66–67
by terrorist groups, 128
trauma and, 71–73, 185
"voluntary" recruitment, 68–70, 72, 85, 87
writing as, 164–170, 184
Reintegration/rehabilitation
advocacy efforts and, 93
of child soldiers, 74–82
by Comic Relief, 138–139
difficulties with, 88, 91–94, 137–138
of displaced persons, 44, 81
evaluating needs for, 179–180
by indigenous cultural practices, 99–101, 103–105
international assistance for, 121–122, 158–161
Renamo (rebel army)
brutality of, 145–146, 148–151
denial of wrongs by, 154
healing practices and, 153
Tinyanga (spirit mediums) and, 103
Resource curse (in DRC), 78
Restoy, Enrique, 20–21
Revolutionary United Front (RUF), 55, 58, 137
Rights of the Child, 94
Rome Statute of the International Criminal Court, 29, 88, 94
Roshani, Niousha, 39–47
Rossi, Andrea, 182
Russia, 23, 26, 116

Russian PKC machine gun, 116
Rwanda
ex-child soldiers in, 176
genocide in, 37
political violence in, 82, 85, 178
reintegrating child soldiers, 80, 175
Rwandan Patriotic Army (RPA), 65

S

al-Sadr, Moqtada, 115, 116
Samarasinghe, Mahinda, 127
Save the Children, 60, 75–77, 80, 81, 142–154
Saveca, Rafael Vicente, 145–146, 153
Security Council (UN), 29
Seko, Mobutu Sese, 35, 82
September 11, 2001, 51
Sexually transmitted diseases (STDs), 57
al-Sheibani, Ahmad, 115, 116
Sheriff, Ansumara, 141
Shia Islamics, 114, 115
Shining Path guerrillas, 55
Sierra Leone, 136–141, 181–188
Sierra Leone, child soldiers
Comic Relief and, 138–139
girls as, 55, 56, 58, 60, 104
indigenous healing rituals of, 105
labor statistics for, 140
poverty and, 71
reintegration difficulties and, 104–105, 132
rights advocacy for, 37, 120, 181–188
survival struggles of, 139–141
U.K. aid to, 136–141
Singer, P. W., 63–73

Sirasu Puli (Leopard Brigade), 65

al-Sistani, Ayatollah Ali, 115

Sitoe, Sangina Salvador, 148

Social, Humanitarian and Cultural Committee (Third Committee), 120–130

Somalia, 35, 133–135, 157

South Africa, 38, 145, 148–150, 174–175

Southern African Development Community (SADC), 123, 124

Spanish Civil War, 92

Sparta, Greece, 16, 87

Speer, Christopher J., 52

SPG 9 rocket launcher, 116

Spies/spying, 157–158, 179

Sri Lanka, child soldiers
    abduction and, 55
    girls as, 56
    international assistance for, 128–129, 186
    parental complicity, 71

St. Petersburg Convention, 84–85

Starvation concerns. *See* Hunger/starvation

Statute of the International Criminal Court, 29, 88, 94

Stearns, Jason, 178

Steinburner, John, 93

Sudan, child soldiers
    initiation ceremonies and, 98
    internally displaced persons in, 40
    international assistance for, 127, 133
    peace process and, 29–30
    recruitment of, 20, 66–67, 157

Sudan People's Liberation Army (SPLA), 65, 66, 73

Suicide missions, 20, 25, 56, 158, 174

Survivor's guilt, 72–73

T

Taliban (terrorist organization), 24–25, 51

Talwar, Namrita, 27–32

Terrorists/terrorism
    al Qaeda, 22, 24–25, 51
    child involvement in, 21–22, 71
    counseling and, 138
    Gitmo and, 51
    guerrilla groups, 42, 90
    recruitment by, 128
    Taliban, 24–25, 51
    See also Renamo

Thematic Work Group, 45

Theseus (Greek hero), 15

Tinyanga (spirit mediums), 103

Trauma concerns
    chemical warfare, 93
    in children, 31–32, 167–168
    dehumanization, 88
    desocialization effects, 88
    domestic violence, 123
    fear tactics, 22–23
    flashback triggers, 92, 167
    indigenous healing and, 99–100, 151–153
    manipulation tactics, 20–21, 37–38
    post-traumatic stress disorder (PTSD), 88, 89, 151, 152
    psychological impact, 57–58, 77, 89, 154–155
    in recruitment tactics, 71–73, 185
    shared collective experience and, 97
    See also Drug abuse; Hunger/starvation; Rape concerns

Trust Fund for Human Security, 129

Turmine, Marion, 81
Tursunova, Zulfiya, 96–105

U

Uganda, 27–32, 171–176
Uganda, child soldiers
  abduction and, 30
  army recruitment in, 22, 172–173
  crisis of, 27–32
  efforts against recruitment, 29–31, 35, 186
  girls as, 20, 171–176
  Lord's Resistance Army in, 27–28, 30, 31, 35, 36, 56, 64
  punishment of, 36
  rehabilitation of, 171–176
  state responsibility for, 133
  trauma concerns, 31–32
  weapons use by, 173–174
Ung, Loung, 164–169
Union des Patriotes Congolais/Reconcialition et Paix (UPC/RP), 64
United Kingdom, 136–141
United Nations (UN)
  Development Programme, 40
  General Assembly, 120–130, 133, 175
  High Commissioner for Refugees (UNHCR), 66, 175
  recruitment age and, 38
  Security Council, 29
  severity of problem and, 108
  Trust Fund for Human Security, 129

See also Convention on the Rights of the Child; International Children's Emergency Fund
United States, 48–53
United States (U.S.), 26, 38, 114
Urban criminal gangs, 86
Uribe, Álvaro, 107, 109

V

Veneman, Ann M., 122, 135
"Voluntary" recruitment, 68–70, 72, 85, 87

W

Wall Street Journal (newspaper), 91
Weapons
  AK-47 automatic rifle, 71, 106, 110, 138
  child use of, 23, 173–174
  children as, in Mozambique, 33–38
  SPG 9 rocket launcher, 116
Withers, Lucia, 108
"Wives" of rebels, 28, 59
Worst Forms of Child Labor Convention, 94

X

Xitlango, Teresa, 151–152, 154

Y

Yemen, child soldiers, 21, 157